Freedom of

CH

ARRANGEM

ACCESS TO INFORMATIO

Right

Section
1. General right of access t
2. Effect of the exemptions
3. Public authorities.
4. Amendment of Schedule ..
5. Further power to designate public authorities.
6. Publicly-owned companies.
7. Public authorities to which Act has limited application.
8. Request for information.
9. Fees.
10. Time for compliance with request.
11. Means by which communication to be made.
12. Exemption where cost of compliance exceeds appropriate limit.
13. Fees for disclosure where cost of compliance exceeds appropriate limit.
14. Vexatious or repeated requests.
15. Special provisions relating to public records transferred to Public Record Office, etc.
16. Duty to provide advice and assistance.

Refusal of request

17. Refusal of request.

The Information Commissioner and the Information Tribunal

18. The Information Commissioner and the Information Tribunal.

Publication schemes

19. Publication schemes
20. Model publication schemes

PART II

EXEMPT INFORMATION

PART III

GENERAL FUNCTIONS OF SECRETARY OF STATE, LORD CHANCELLOR AND INFORMATION COMMISSIONER

PART IV

ENFORCEMENT

PART V

APPEALS

Freedom of Information Act 2000

2000 CHAPTER 36

An Act to make provision for the disclosure of information held by public authorities or by persons providing services for them and to amend the Data Protection Act 1998 and the Public Records Act 1958; and for connected purposes.   [30th November 2000]

BE IT ENACTED by the Queen's most Excellent Majesty, by and with the advice and consent of the Lords Spiritual and Temporal, and Commons, in this present Parliament assembled, and by the authority of the same, as follows:—

PART I

ACCESS TO INFORMATION HELD BY PUBLIC AUTHORITIES

Right to information

1.—(1) Any person making a request for information to a public authority is entitled—

    (a) to be informed in writing by the public authority whether it holds information of the description specified in the request, and

    (b) if that is the case, to have that information communicated to him.

General right of access to information held by public authorities.

(2) Subsection (1) has effect subject to the following provisions of this section and to the provisions of sections 2, 9, 12 and 14.

(3) Where a public authority—

    (a) reasonably requires further information in order to identify and locate the information requested, and

    (b) has informed the applicant of that requirement,

the authority is not obliged to comply with subsection (1) unless it is supplied with that further information.

(4) The information—

    (a) in respect of which the applicant is to be informed under subsection (1)(a), or

    (b) which is to be communicated under subsection (1)(b),

is the information in question held at the time when the request is received, except that account may be taken of any amendment or deletion made between that time and the time when the information is to be communicated under subsection (1)(b), being an amendment or deletion that would have been made regardless of the receipt of the request.

(5) A public authority is to be taken to have complied with subsection (1)(a) in relation to any information if it has communicated the information to the applicant in accordance with subsection (1)(b).

(6) In this Act, the duty of a public authority to comply with subsection (1)(a) is referred to as "the duty to confirm or deny".

Effect of the exemptions in Part II.

2.—(1) Where any provision of Part II states that the duty to confirm or deny does not arise in relation to any information, the effect of the provision is that where either—

    (a) the provision confers absolute exemption, or

    (b) in all the circumstances of the case, the public interest in maintaining the exclusion of the duty to confirm or deny outweighs the public interest in disclosing whether the public authority holds the information,

section 1(1)(a) does not apply.

(2) In respect of any information which is exempt information by virtue of any provision of Part II, section 1(1)(b) does not apply if or to the extent that—

    (a) the information is exempt information by virtue of a provision conferring absolute exemption, or

    (b) in all the circumstances of the case, the public interest in maintaining the exemption outweighs the public interest in disclosing the information.

(3) For the purposes of this section, the following provisions of Part II (and no others) are to be regarded as conferring absolute exemption—

    (a) section 21,

    (b) section 23,

    (c) section 32,

    (d) section 34,

    (e) section 36 so far as relating to information held by the House of Commons or the House of Lords,

    (f) in section 40—

        (i) subsection (1), and

        (ii) subsection (2) so far as relating to cases where the first condition referred to in that subsection is satisfied by virtue of subsection (3)(a)(i) or (b) of that section,

    (g) section 41, and

    (h) section 44.

3.—(1) In this Act "public authority" means—

(a) subject to section 4(4), any body which, any other person who, or the holder of any office which—

    (i) is listed in Schedule 1, or

    (ii) is designated by order under section 5, or

(b) a publicly-owned company as defined by section 6.

(2) For the purposes of this Act, information is held by a public authority if—

(a) it is held by the authority, otherwise than on behalf of another person, or

(b) it is held by another person on behalf of the authority.

4.—(1) The Secretary of State may by order amend Schedule 1 by adding to that Schedule a reference to any body or the holder of any office which (in either case) is not for the time being listed in that Schedule but as respects which both the first and the second conditions below are satisfied. Amendment of Schedule 1.

(2) The first condition is that the body or office—

(a) is established by virtue of Her Majesty's prerogative or by an enactment or by subordinate legislation, or

(b) is established in any other way by a Minister of the Crown in his capacity as Minister, by a government department or by the National Assembly for Wales.

(3) The second condition is—

(a) in the case of a body, that the body is wholly or partly constituted by appointment made by the Crown, by a Minister of the Crown, by a government department or by the National Assembly for Wales, or

(b) in the case of an office, that appointments to the office are made by the Crown, by a Minister of the Crown, by a government department or by the National Assembly for Wales.

(4) If either the first or the second condition above ceases to be satisfied as respects any body or office which is listed in Part VI or VII of Schedule 1, that body or the holder of that office shall cease to be a public authority by virtue of the entry in question.

(5) The Secretary of State may by order amend Schedule 1 by removing from Part VI or VII of that Schedule an entry relating to any body or office—

(a) which has ceased to exist, or

(b) as respects which either the first or the second condition above has ceased to be satisfied.

(6) An order under subsection (1) may relate to a specified person or office or to persons or offices falling within a specified description.

(7) Before making an order under subsection (1), the Secretary of State shall—

(a) if the order adds to Part II, III, IV or VI of Schedule 1 a reference to—

    (i) a body whose functions are exercisable only or mainly in or as regards Wales, or

(ii) the holder of an office whose functions are exercisable only or mainly in or as regards Wales,

consult the National Assembly for Wales, and

(b) if the order relates to a body which, or the holder of any office who, if the order were made, would be a Northern Ireland public authority, consult the First Minister and deputy First Minister in Northern Ireland.

(8) This section has effect subject to section 80.

(9) In this section "Minister of the Crown" includes a Northern Ireland Minister.

Further power to designate public authorities.

5.—(1) The Secretary of State may by order designate as a public authority for the purposes of this Act any person who is neither listed in Schedule 1 nor capable of being added to that Schedule by an order under section 4(1), but who—

(a) appears to the Secretary of State to exercise functions of a public nature, or

(b) is providing under a contract made with a public authority any service whose provision is a function of that authority.

(2) An order under this section may designate a specified person or office or persons or offices falling within a specified description.

(3) Before making an order under this section, the Secretary of State shall consult every person to whom the order relates, or persons appearing to him to represent such persons.

(4) This section has effect subject to section 80.

Publicly-owned companies.

6.—(1) A company is a "publicly-owned company" for the purposes of section 3(1)(b) if—

(a) it is wholly owned by the Crown, or

(b) it is wholly owned by any public authority listed in Schedule 1 other than—

(i) a government department, or

(ii) any authority which is listed only in relation to particular information.

(2) For the purposes of this section—

(a) a company is wholly owned by the Crown if it has no members except—

(i) Ministers of the Crown, government departments or companies wholly owned by the Crown, or

(ii) persons acting on behalf of Ministers of the Crown, government departments or companies wholly owned by the Crown, and

(b) a company is wholly owned by a public authority other than a government department if it has no members except—

(i) that public authority or companies wholly owned by that public authority, or

(ii) persons acting on behalf of that public authority or of companies wholly owned by that public authority.

(3) In this section—

"company" includes any body corporate;

"Minister of the Crown" includes a Northern Ireland Minister.

7.—(1) Where a public authority is listed in Schedule 1 only in relation to information of a specified description, nothing in Parts I to V of this Act applies to any other information held by the authority.

(2) An order under section 4(1) may, in adding an entry to Schedule 1, list the public authority only in relation to information of a specified description.

(3) The Secretary of State may by order amend Schedule 1—

(a) by limiting to information of a specified description the entry relating to any public authority, or

(b) by removing or amending any limitation to information of a specified description which is for the time being contained in any entry.

(4) Before making an order under subsection (3), the Secretary of State shall—

(a) if the order relates to the National Assembly for Wales or a Welsh public authority, consult the National Assembly for Wales,

(b) if the order relates to the Northern Ireland Assembly, consult the Presiding Officer of that Assembly, and

(c) if the order relates to a Northern Ireland department or a Northern Ireland public authority, consult the First Minister and deputy First Minister in Northern Ireland.

(5) An order under section 5(1)(a) must specify the functions of the public authority designated by the order with respect to which the designation is to have effect; and nothing in Parts I to V of this Act applies to information which is held by the authority but does not relate to the exercise of those functions.

(6) An order under section 5(1)(b) must specify the services provided under contract with respect to which the designation is to have effect; and nothing in Parts I to V of this Act applies to information which is held by the public authority designated by the order but does not relate to the provision of those services.

(7) Nothing in Parts I to V of this Act applies in relation to any information held by a publicly-owned company which is excluded information in relation to that company.

(8) In subsection (7) "excluded information", in relation to a publicly-owned company, means information which is of a description specified in relation to that company in an order made by the Secretary of State for the purposes of this subsection.

(9) In this section "publicly-owned company" has the meaning given by section 6.

8.—(1) In this Act any reference to a "request for information" is a reference to such a request which—

(a) is in writing,

Public authorities to which Act has limited application.

Request for information.

(b) states the name of the applicant and an address for correspondence, and

(c) describes the information requested.

(2) For the purposes of subsection (1)(a), a request is to be treated as made in writing where the text of the request—

(a) is transmitted by electronic means,

(b) is received in legible form, and

(c) is capable of being used for subsequent reference.

Fees.

9.—(1) A public authority to whom a request for information is made may, within the period for complying with section 1(1), give the applicant a notice in writing (in this Act referred to as a "fees notice") stating that a fee of an amount specified in the notice is to be charged by the authority for complying with section 1(1).

(2) Where a fees notice has been given to the applicant, the public authority is not obliged to comply with section 1(1) unless the fee is paid within the period of three months beginning with the day on which the fees notice is given to the applicant.

(3) Subject to subsection (5), any fee under this section must be determined by the public authority in accordance with regulations made by the Secretary of State.

(4) Regulations under subsection (3) may, in particular, provide—

(a) that no fee is to be payable in prescribed cases,

(b) that any fee is not to exceed such maximum as may be specified in, or determined in accordance with, the regulations, and

(c) that any fee is to be calculated in such manner as may be prescribed by the regulations.

(5) Subsection (3) does not apply where provision is made by or under any enactment as to the fee that may be charged by the public authority for the disclosure of the information.

Time for compliance with request.

10.—(1) Subject to subsections (2) and (3), a public authority must comply with section 1(1) promptly and in any event not later than the twentieth working day following the date of receipt.

(2) Where the authority has given a fees notice to the applicant and the fee is paid in accordance with section 9(2), the working days in the period beginning with the day on which the fees notice is given to the applicant and ending with the day on which the fee is received by the authority are to be disregarded in calculating for the purposes of subsection (1) the twentieth working day following the date of receipt.

(3) If, and to the extent that—

(a) section 1(1)(a) would not apply if the condition in section 2(1)(b) were satisfied, or

(b) section 1(1)(b) would not apply if the condition in section 2(2)(b) were satisfied,

the public authority need not comply with section 1(1)(a) or (b) until such time as is reasonable in the circumstances; but this subsection does not affect the time by which any notice under section 17(1) must be given.

(4) The Secretary of State may by regulations provide that subsections (1) and (2) are to have effect as if any reference to the twentieth working day following the date of receipt were a reference to such other day, not later than the sixtieth working day following the date of receipt, as may be specified in, or determined in accordance with, the regulations.

(5) Regulations under subsection (4) may—

(a) prescribe different days in relation to different cases, and

(b) confer a discretion on the Commissioner.

(6) In this section—

"the date of receipt" means—

(a) the day on which the public authority receives the request for information, or

(b) if later, the day on which it receives the information referred to in section 1(3);

"working day" means any day other than a Saturday, a Sunday, Christmas Day, Good Friday or a day which is a bank holiday under the Banking and Financial Dealings Act 1971 in any part of the United Kingdom.

1971 c. 80.

11.—(1) Where, on making his request for information, the applicant expresses a preference for communication by any one or more of the following means, namely—

Means by which communication to be made.

(a) the provision to the applicant of a copy of the information in permanent form or in another form acceptable to the applicant,

(b) the provision to the applicant of a reasonable opportunity to inspect a record containing the information, and

(c) the provision to the applicant of a digest or summary of the information in permanent form or in another form acceptable to the applicant,

the public authority shall so far as reasonably practicable give effect to that preference.

(2) In determining for the purposes of this section whether it is reasonably practicable to communicate information by particular means, the public authority may have regard to all the circumstances, including the cost of doing so.

(3) Where the public authority determines that it is not reasonably practicable to comply with any preference expressed by the applicant in making his request, the authority shall notify the applicant of the reasons for its determination.

(4) Subject to subsection (1), a public authority may comply with a request by communicating information by any means which are reasonable in the circumstances.

12.—(1) Section 1(1) does not oblige a public authority to comply with a request for information if the authority estimates that the cost of complying with the request would exceed the appropriate limit.

Exemption where cost of compliance exceeds appropriate limit.

(2) Subsection (1) does not exempt the public authority from its obligation to comply with paragraph (a) of section 1(1) unless the estimated cost of complying with that paragraph alone would exceed the appropriate limit.

(3) In subsections (1) and (2) "the appropriate limit" means such amount as may be prescribed, and different amounts may be prescribed in relation to different cases.

(4) The Secretary of State may by regulations provide that, in such circumstances as may be prescribed, where two or more requests for information are made to a public authority—

    (a) by one person, or

    (b) by different persons who appear to the public authority to be acting in concert or in pursuance of a campaign,

the estimated cost of complying with any of the requests is to be taken to be the estimated total cost of complying with all of them.

(5) The Secretary of State may by regulations make provision for the purposes of this section as to the costs to be estimated and as to the manner in which they are to be estimated.

Fees for disclosure where cost of compliance exceeds appropriate limit.

13.—(1) A public authority may charge for the communication of any information whose communication—

    (a) is not required by section 1(1) because the cost of complying with the request for information exceeds the amount which is the appropriate limit for the purposes of section 12(1) and (2), and

    (b) is not otherwise required by law,

such fee as may be determined by the public authority in accordance with regulations made by the Secretary of State.

(2) Regulations under this section may, in particular, provide—

    (a) that any fee is not to exceed such maximum as may be specified in, or determined in accordance with, the regulations, and

    (b) that any fee is to be calculated in such manner as may be prescribed by the regulations.

(3) Subsection (1) does not apply where provision is made by or under any enactment as to the fee that may be charged by the public authority for the disclosure of the information.

Vexatious or repeated requests.

14.—(1) Section 1(1) does not oblige a public authority to comply with a request for information if the request is vexatious.

(2) Where a public authority has previously complied with a request for information which was made by any person, it is not obliged to comply with a subsequent identical or substantially similar request from that person unless a reasonable interval has elapsed between compliance with the previous request and the making of the current request.

Special provisions relating to public records transferred to Public Record Office, etc.

15.—(1) Where—

    (a) the appropriate records authority receives a request for information which relates to information which is, or if it existed would be, contained in a transferred public record, and

(b) either of the conditions in subsection (2) is satisfied in relation to any of that information,

that authority shall, within the period for complying with section 1(1), send a copy of the request to the responsible authority.

(2) The conditions referred to in subsection (1)(b) are—

(a) that the duty to confirm or deny is expressed to be excluded only by a provision of Part II not specified in subsection (3) of section 2, and

(b) that the information is exempt information only by virtue of a provision of Part II not specified in that subsection.

(3) On receiving the copy, the responsible authority shall, within such time as is reasonable in all the circumstances, inform the appropriate records authority of the determination required by virtue of subsection (3) or (4) of section 66.

(4) In this Act "transferred public record" means a public record which has been transferred—

(a) to the Public Record Office,

(b) to another place of deposit appointed by the Lord Chancellor under the Public Records Act 1958, or

1958 c. 51.

(c) to the Public Record Office of Northern Ireland.

(5) In this Act—

"appropriate records authority", in relation to a transferred public record, means—

(a) in a case falling within subsection (4)(a), the Public Record Office,

(b) in a case falling within subsection (4)(b), the Lord Chancellor, and

(c) in a case falling within subsection (4)(c), the Public Record Office of Northern Ireland;

"responsible authority", in relation to a transferred public record, means—

(a) in the case of a record transferred as mentioned in subsection (4)(a) or (b) from a government department in the charge of a Minister of the Crown, the Minister of the Crown who appears to the Lord Chancellor to be primarily concerned,

(b) in the case of a record transferred as mentioned in subsection (4)(a) or (b) from any other person, the person who appears to the Lord Chancellor to be primarily concerned,

(c) in the case of a record transferred to the Public Record Office of Northern Ireland from a government department in the charge of a Minister of the Crown, the Minister of the Crown who appears to the appropriate Northern Ireland Minister to be primarily concerned,

(d) in the case of a record transferred to the Public Record Office of Northern Ireland from a Northern Ireland department, the Northern Ireland Minister who appears to the appropriate Northern Ireland Minister to be primarily concerned, or

(e) in the case of a record transferred to the Public Record Office of Northern Ireland from any other person, the person who appears to the appropriate Northern Ireland Minister to be primarily concerned.

Duty to provide advice and assistance.

16.—(1) It shall be the duty of a public authority to provide advice and assistance, so far as it would be reasonable to expect the authority to do so, to persons who propose to make, or have made, requests for information to it.

(2) Any public authority which, in relation to the provision of advice or assistance in any case, conforms with the code of practice under section 45 is to be taken to comply with the duty imposed by subsection (1) in relation to that case.

Refusal of request

Refusal of request.

17.—(1) A public authority which, in relation to any request for information, is to any extent relying on a claim that any provision of Part II relating to the duty to confirm or deny is relevant to the request or on a claim that information is exempt information must, within the time for complying with section 1(1), give the applicant a notice which—

(a) states that fact,

(b) specifies the exemption in question, and

(c) states (if that would not otherwise be apparent) why the exemption applies.

(2) Where—

(a) in relation to any request for information, a public authority is, as respects any information, relying on a claim—

(i) that any provision of Part II which relates to the duty to confirm or deny and is not specified in section 2(3) is relevant to the request, or

(ii) that the information is exempt information only by virtue of a provision not specified in section 2(3), and

(b) at the time when the notice under subsection (1) is given to the applicant, the public authority (or, in a case falling within section 66(3) or (4), the responsible authority) has not yet reached a decision as to the application of subsection (1)(b) or (2)(b) of section 2,

the notice under subsection (1) must indicate that no decision as to the application of that provision has yet been reached and must contain an estimate of the date by which the authority expects that such a decision will have been reached.

(3) A public authority which, in relation to any request for information, is to any extent relying on a claim that subsection (1)(b) or (2)(b) of section 2 applies must, either in the notice under subsection (1) or in a separate notice given within such time as is reasonable in the circumstances, state the reasons for claiming—

(a) that, in all the circumstances of the case, the public interest in maintaining the exclusion of the duty to confirm or deny outweighs the public interest in disclosing whether the authority holds the information, or

(b) that, in all the circumstances of the case, the public interest in maintaining the exemption outweighs the public interest in disclosing the information.

(4) A public authority is not obliged to make a statement under subsection (1)(c) or (3) if, or to the extent that, the statement would involve the disclosure of information which would itself be exempt information.

(5) A public authority which, in relation to any request for information, is relying on a claim that section 12 or 14 applies must, within the time for complying with section 1(1), give the applicant a notice stating that fact.

(6) Subsection (5) does not apply where—

(a) the public authority is relying on a claim that section 14 applies,

(b) the authority has given the applicant a notice, in relation to a previous request for information, stating that it is relying on such a claim, and

(c) it would in all the circumstances be unreasonable to expect the authority to serve a further notice under subsection (5) in relation to the current request.

(7) A notice under subsection (1), (3) or (5) must—

(a) contain particulars of any procedure provided by the public authority for dealing with complaints about the handling of requests for information or state that the authority does not provide such a procedure, and

(b) contain particulars of the right conferred by section 50.

The Information Commissioner and the Information Tribunal

18.—(1) The Data Protection Commissioner shall be known instead as the Information Commissioner.

(2) The Data Protection Tribunal shall be known instead as the Information Tribunal.

(3) In this Act—

(a) the Information Commissioner is referred to as "the Commissioner", and

(b) the Information Tribunal is referred to as "the Tribunal".

(4) Schedule 2 (which makes provision consequential on subsections (1) and (2) and amendments of the Data Protection Act 1998 relating to the extension by this Act of the functions of the Commissioner and the Tribunal) has effect.

(5) If the person who held office as Data Protection Commissioner immediately before the day on which this Act is passed remains in office as Information Commissioner at the end of the period of two years beginning with that day, he shall vacate his office at the end of that period.

(6) Subsection (5) does not prevent the re-appointment of a person whose appointment is terminated by that subsection.

(7) In the application of paragraph 2(4)(b) and (5) of Schedule 5 to the Data Protection Act 1998 (Commissioner not to serve for more than fifteen years and not to be appointed, except in special circumstances, for

Marginal notes:

The Information Commissioner and the Information Tribunal.

1998 c. 29.

PART I

a third or subsequent term) to anything done after the passing of this Act, there shall be left out of account any term of office served by virtue of an appointment made before the passing of this Act.

Publication schemes

Publication schemes.

19.—(1) It shall be the duty of every public authority—

(a) to adopt and maintain a scheme which relates to the publication of information by the authority and is approved by the Commissioner (in this Act referred to as a "publication scheme"),

(b) to publish information in accordance with its publication scheme, and

(c) from time to time to review its publication scheme.

(2) A publication scheme must—

(a) specify classes of information which the public authority publishes or intends to publish,

(b) specify the manner in which information of each class is, or is intended to be, published, and

(c) specify whether the material is, or is intended to be, available to the public free of charge or on payment.

(3) In adopting or reviewing a publication scheme, a public authority shall have regard to the public interest—

(a) in allowing public access to information held by the authority, and

(b) in the publication of reasons for decisions made by the authority.

(4) A public authority shall publish its publication scheme in such manner as it thinks fit.

(5) The Commissioner may, when approving a scheme, provide that his approval is to expire at the end of a specified period.

(6) Where the Commissioner has approved the publication scheme of any public authority, he may at any time give notice to the public authority revoking his approval of the scheme as from the end of the period of six months beginning with the day on which the notice is given.

(7) Where the Commissioner—

(a) refuses to approve a proposed publication scheme, or

(b) revokes his approval of a publication scheme,

he must give the public authority a statement of his reasons for doing so.

Model publication schemes.

20.—(1) The Commissioner may from time to time approve, in relation to public authorities falling within particular classes, model publication schemes prepared by him or by other persons.

(2) Where a public authority falling within the class to which an approved model scheme relates adopts such a scheme without modification, no further approval of the Commissioner is required so long as the model scheme remains approved; and where such an authority adopts such a scheme with modifications, the approval of the Commissioner is required only in relation to the modifications.

(3) The Commissioner may, when approving a model publication scheme, provide that his approval is to expire at the end of a specified period.

(4) Where the Commissioner has approved a model publication scheme, he may at any time publish, in such manner as he thinks fit, a notice revoking his approval of the scheme as from the end of the period of six months beginning with the day on which the notice is published.

(5) Where the Commissioner refuses to approve a proposed model publication scheme on the application of any person, he must give the person who applied for approval of the scheme a statement of the reasons for his refusal.

(6) Where the Commissioner refuses to approve any modifications under subsection (2), he must give the public authority a statement of the reasons for his refusal.

(7) Where the Commissioner revokes his approval of a model publication scheme, he must include in the notice under subsection (4) a statement of his reasons for doing so.

PART II

EXEMPT INFORMATION

21.—(1) Information which is reasonably accessible to the applicant otherwise than under section 1 is exempt information.

Information accessible to applicant by other means.

(2) For the purposes of subsection (1)—

    (a) information may be reasonably accessible to the applicant even though it is accessible only on payment, and

    (b) information is to be taken to be reasonably accessible to the applicant if it is information which the public authority or any other person is obliged by or under any enactment to communicate (otherwise than by making the information available for inspection) to members of the public on request, whether free of charge or on payment.

(3) For the purposes of subsection (1), information which is held by a public authority and does not fall within subsection (2)(b) is not to be regarded as reasonably accessible to the applicant merely because the information is available from the public authority itself on request, unless the information is made available in accordance with the authority's publication scheme and any payment required is specified in, or determined in accordance with, the scheme.

22.—(1) Information is exempt information if—

Information intended for future publication.

    (a) the information is held by the public authority with a view to its publication, by the authority or any other person, at some future date (whether determined or not),

    (b) the information was already held with a view to such publication at the time when the request for information was made, and

    (c) it is reasonable in all the circumstances that the information should be withheld from disclosure until the date referred to in paragraph (a).

(2) The duty to confirm or deny does not arise if, or to the extent that, compliance with section 1(1)(a) would involve the disclosure of any information (whether or not already recorded) which falls within subsection (1).

Information supplied by, or relating to, bodies dealing with security matters.

23.—(1) Information held by a public authority is exempt information if it was directly or indirectly supplied to the public authority by, or relates to, any of the bodies specified in subsection (3).

(2) A certificate signed by a Minister of the Crown certifying that the information to which it applies was directly or indirectly supplied by, or relates to, any of the bodies specified in subsection (3) shall, subject to section 60, be conclusive evidence of that fact.

(3) The bodies referred to in subsections (1) and (2) are—

(a) the Security Service,

(b) the Secret Intelligence Service,

(c) the Government Communications Headquarters,

(d) the special forces,

2000 c. 23.

(e) the Tribunal established under section 65 of the Regulation of Investigatory Powers Act 2000,

1985 c. 56.

(f) the Tribunal established under section 7 of the Interception of Communications Act 1985,

1989 c. 5.

(g) the Tribunal established under section 5 of the Security Service Act 1989,

1994 c. 13.

(h) the Tribunal established under section 9 of the Intelligence Services Act 1994,

(i) the Security Vetting Appeals Panel,

(j) the Security Commission,

(k) the National Criminal Intelligence Service, and

(l) the Service Authority for the National Criminal Intelligence Service.

(4) In subsection (3)(c) "the Government Communications Headquarters" includes any unit or part of a unit of the armed forces of the Crown which is for the time being required by the Secretary of State to assist the Government Communications Headquarters in carrying out its functions.

(5) The duty to confirm or deny does not arise if, or to the extent that, compliance with section 1(1)(a) would involve the disclosure of any information (whether or not already recorded) which was directly or indirectly supplied to the public authority by, or relates to, any of the bodies specified in subsection (3).

National security.

24.—(1) Information which does not fall within section 23(1) is exempt information if exemption from section 1(1)(b) is required for the purpose of safeguarding national security.

(2) The duty to confirm or deny does not arise if, or to the extent that, exemption from section 1(1)(a) is required for the purpose of safeguarding national security.

(3) A certificate signed by a Minister of the Crown certifying that exemption from section 1(1)(b), or from section 1(1)(a) and (b), is, or at any time was, required for the purpose of safeguarding national security shall, subject to section 60, be conclusive evidence of that fact.

(4) A certificate under subsection (3) may identify the information to which it applies by means of a general description and may be expressed to have prospective effect.

25.—(1) A document purporting to be a certificate under section 23(2) or 24(3) shall be received in evidence and deemed to be such a certificate unless the contrary is proved.

(2) A document which purports to be certified by or on behalf of a Minister of the Crown as a true copy of a certificate issued by that Minister under section 23(2) or 24(3) shall in any legal proceedings be evidence (or, in Scotland, sufficient evidence) of that certificate.

(3) The power conferred by section 23(2) or 24(3) on a Minister of the Crown shall not be exercisable except by a Minister who is a member of the Cabinet or by the Attorney General, the Advocate General for Scotland or the Attorney General for Northern Ireland.

26.—(1) Information is exempt information if its disclosure under this Act would, or would be likely to, prejudice—

Defence.

   (a) the defence of the British Islands or of any colony, or

   (b) the capability, effectiveness or security of any relevant forces.

(2) In subsection (1)(b) "relevant forces" means—

   (a) the armed forces of the Crown, and

   (b) any forces co-operating with those forces,

or any part of any of those forces.

(3) The duty to confirm or deny does not arise if, or to the extent that, compliance with section 1(1)(a) would, or would be likely to, prejudice any of the matters mentioned in subsection (1).

27.—(1) Information is exempt information if its disclosure under this Act would, or would be likely to, prejudice—

International relations.

   (a) relations between the United Kingdom and any other State,

   (b) relations between the United Kingdom and any international organisation or international court,

   (c) the interests of the United Kingdom abroad, or

   (d) the promotion or protection by the United Kingdom of its interests abroad.

(2) Information is also exempt information if it is confidential information obtained from a State other than the United Kingdom or from an international organisation or international court.

(3) For the purposes of this section, any information obtained from a State, organisation or court is confidential at any time while the terms on which it was obtained require it to be held in confidence or while the circumstances in which it was obtained make it reasonable for the State, organisation or court to expect that it will be so held.

(4) The duty to confirm or deny does not arise if, or to the extent that, compliance with section 1(1)(a)—

    (a) would, or would be likely to, prejudice any of the matters mentioned in subsection (1), or

    (b) would involve the disclosure of any information (whether or not already recorded) which is confidential information obtained from a State other than the United Kingdom or from an international organisation or international court.

(5) In this section—

"international court" means any international court which is not an international organisation and which is established—

      (a) by a resolution of an international organisation of which the United Kingdom is a member, or

      (b) by an international agreement to which the United Kingdom is a party;

"international organisation" means any international organisation whose members include any two or more States, or any organ of such an organisation;

"State" includes the government of any State and any organ of its government, and references to a State other than the United Kingdom include references to any territory outside the United Kingdom.

Relations within the United Kingdom.

28.—(1) Information is exempt information if its disclosure under this Act would, or would be likely to, prejudice relations between any administration in the United Kingdom and any other such administration.

(2) In subsection (1) "administration in the United Kingdom" means—

    (a) the government of the United Kingdom,

    (b) the Scottish Administration,

    (c) the Executive Committee of the Northern Ireland Assembly, or

    (d) the National Assembly for Wales.

(3) The duty to confirm or deny does not arise if, or to the extent that, compliance with section 1(1)(a) would, or would be likely to, prejudice any of the matters mentioned in subsection (1).

The economy.

29.—(1) Information is exempt information if its disclosure under this Act would, or would be likely to, prejudice—

    (a) the economic interests of the United Kingdom or of any part of the United Kingdom, or

    (b) the financial interests of any administration in the United Kingdom, as defined by section 28(2).

(2) The duty to confirm or deny does not arise if, or to the extent that, compliance with section 1(1)(a) would, or would be likely to, prejudice any of the matters mentioned in subsection (1).

Investigations and proceedings conducted by public authorities.

30.—(1) Information held by a public authority is exempt information if it has at any time been held by the authority for the purposes of—

    (a) any investigation which the public authority has a duty to conduct with a view to it being ascertained—

        (i) whether a person should be charged with an offence, or

        (ii) whether a person charged with an offence is guilty of it,

    (b) any investigation which is conducted by the authority and in the circumstances may lead to a decision by the authority to institute criminal proceedings which the authority has power to conduct, or

    (c) any criminal proceedings which the authority has power to conduct.

  (2) Information held by a public authority is exempt information if—

    (a) it was obtained or recorded by the authority for the purposes of its functions relating to—

        (i) investigations falling within subsection (1)(a) or (b),

        (ii) criminal proceedings which the authority has power to conduct,

        (iii) investigations (other than investigations falling within subsection (1)(a) or (b)) which are conducted by the authority for any of the purposes specified in section 31(2) and either by virtue of Her Majesty's prerogative or by virtue of powers conferred by or under any enactment, or

        (iv) civil proceedings which are brought by or on behalf of the authority and arise out of such investigations, and

    (b) it relates to the obtaining of information from confidential sources.

  (3) The duty to confirm or deny does not arise in relation to information which is (or if it were held by the public authority would be) exempt information by virtue of subsection (1) or (2).

  (4) In relation to the institution or conduct of criminal proceedings or the power to conduct them, references in subsection (1)(b) or (c) and subsection (2)(a) to the public authority include references—

    (a) to any officer of the authority,

    (b) in the case of a government department other than a Northern Ireland department, to the Minister of the Crown in charge of the department, and

    (c) in the case of a Northern Ireland department, to the Northern Ireland Minister in charge of the department.

  (5) In this section—

"criminal proceedings" includes—

      (a) proceedings before a court-martial constituted under the Army Act 1955, the Air Force Act 1955 or the Naval Discipline Act 1957 or a disciplinary court constituted under section 52G of the Act of 1957,

      (b) proceedings on dealing summarily with a charge under the Army Act 1955 or the Air Force Act 1955 or on summary trial under the Naval Discipline Act 1957,

1955 c. 18.
1955 c. 19.
1957 c. 53.

Part II

1955 c. 18.
1955 c. 19.
1957 c. 53.

(c) proceedings before a court established by section 83ZA of the Army Act 1955, section 83ZA of the Air Force Act 1955 or section 52FF of the Naval Discipline Act 1957 (summary appeal courts),

(d) proceedings before the Courts-Martial Appeal Court, and

(e) proceedings before a Standing Civilian Court;

"offence" includes any offence under the Army Act 1955, the Air Force Act 1955 or the Naval Discipline Act 1957.

(6) In the application of this section to Scotland—

(a) in subsection (1)(b), for the words from "a decision" to the end there is substituted "a decision by the authority to make a report to the procurator fiscal for the purpose of enabling him to determine whether criminal proceedings should be instituted",

(b) in subsections (1)(c) and (2)(a)(ii) for "which the authority has power to conduct" there is substituted "which have been instituted in consequence of a report made by the authority to the procurator fiscal", and

(c) for any reference to a person being charged with an offence there is substituted a reference to the person being prosecuted for the offence.

Law enforcement.

31.—(1) Information which is not exempt information by virtue of section 30 is exempt information if its disclosure under this Act would, or would be likely to, prejudice—

(a) the prevention or detection of crime,

(b) the apprehension or prosecution of offenders,

(c) the administration of justice,

(d) the assessment or collection of any tax or duty or of any imposition of a similar nature,

(e) the operation of the immigration controls,

(f) the maintenance of security and good order in prisons or in other institutions where persons are lawfully detained,

(g) the exercise by any public authority of its functions for any of the purposes specified in subsection (2),

(h) any civil proceedings which are brought by or on behalf of a public authority and arise out of an investigation conducted, for any of the purposes specified in subsection (2), by or on behalf of the authority by virtue of Her Majesty's prerogative or by virtue of powers conferred by or under an enactment, or

1976 c. 14.

(i) any inquiry held under the Fatal Accidents and Sudden Deaths Inquiries (Scotland) Act 1976 to the extent that the inquiry arises out of an investigation conducted, for any of the purposes specified in subsection (2), by or on behalf of the authority by virtue of Her Majesty's prerogative or by virtue of powers conferred by or under an enactment.

(2) The purposes referred to in subsection (1)(g) to (i) are—

(a) the purpose of ascertaining whether any person has failed to comply with the law,

(b) the purpose of ascertaining whether any person is responsible for any conduct which is improper,

(c) the purpose of ascertaining whether circumstances which would justify regulatory action in pursuance of any enactment exist or may arise,

(d) the purpose of ascertaining a person's fitness or competence in relation to the management of bodies corporate or in relation to any profession or other activity which he is, or seeks to become, authorised to carry on,

(e) the purpose of ascertaining the cause of an accident,

(f) the purpose of protecting charities against misconduct or mismanagement (whether by trustees or other persons) in their administration,

(g) the purpose of protecting the property of charities from loss or misapplication,

(h) the purpose of recovering the property of charities,

(i) the purpose of securing the health, safety and welfare of persons at work, and

(j) the purpose of protecting persons other than persons at work against risk to health or safety arising out of or in connection with the actions of persons at work.

(3) The duty to confirm or deny does not arise if, or to the extent that, compliance with section 1(1)(a) would, or would be likely to, prejudice any of the matters mentioned in subsection (1).

32.—(1) Information held by a public authority is exempt information if it is held only by virtue of being contained in— Court records, etc.

(a) any document filed with, or otherwise placed in the custody of, a court for the purposes of proceedings in a particular cause or matter,

(b) any document served upon, or by, a public authority for the purposes of proceedings in a particular cause or matter, or

(c) any document created by—

   (i) a court, or

   (ii) a member of the administrative staff of a court,

for the purposes of proceedings in a particular cause or matter.

(2) Information held by a public authority is exempt information if it is held only by virtue of being contained in—

(a) any document placed in the custody of a person conducting an inquiry or arbitration, for the purposes of the inquiry or arbitration, or

(b) any document created by a person conducting an inquiry or arbitration, for the purposes of the inquiry or arbitration.

(3) The duty to confirm or deny does not arise in relation to information which is (or if it were held by the public authority would be) exempt information by virtue of this section.

(4) In this section—

(a) "court" includes any tribunal or body exercising the judicial power of the State,

(b) "proceedings in a particular cause or matter" includes any inquest or post-mortem examination,

(c) "inquiry" means any inquiry or hearing held under any provision contained in, or made under, an enactment, and

1996 c. 23.

(d) except in relation to Scotland, "arbitration" means any arbitration to which Part I of the Arbitration Act 1996 applies.

Audit functions.

33.—(1) This section applies to any public authority which has functions in relation to—

(a) the audit of the accounts of other public authorities, or

(b) the examination of the economy, efficiency and effectiveness with which other public authorities use their resources in discharging their functions.

(2) Information held by a public authority to which this section applies is exempt information if its disclosure would, or would be likely to, prejudice the exercise of any of the authority's functions in relation to any of the matters referred to in subsection (1).

(3) The duty to confirm or deny does not arise in relation to a public authority to which this section applies if, or to the extent that, compliance with section 1(1)(a) would, or would be likely to, prejudice the exercise of any of the authority's functions in relation to any of the matters referred to in subsection (1).

Parliamentary privilege.

34.—(1) Information is exempt information if exemption from section 1(1)(b) is required for the purpose of avoiding an infringement of the privileges of either House of Parliament.

(2) The duty to confirm or deny does not apply if, or to the extent that, exemption from section 1(1)(a) is required for the purpose of avoiding an infringement of the privileges of either House of Parliament.

(3) A certificate signed by the appropriate authority certifying that exemption from section 1(1)(b), or from section 1(1)(a) and (b), is, or at any time was, required for the purpose of avoiding an infringement of the privileges of either House of Parliament shall be conclusive evidence of that fact.

(4) In subsection (3) "the appropriate authority" means—

(a) in relation to the House of Commons, the Speaker of that House, and

(b) in relation to the House of Lords, the Clerk of the Parliaments.

Formulation of government policy, etc.

35.—(1) Information held by a government department or by the National Assembly for Wales is exempt information if it relates to—

(a) the formulation or development of government policy,

(b) Ministerial communications,

(c) the provision of advice by any of the Law Officers or any request for the provision of such advice, or

(d) the operation of any Ministerial private office.

(2) Once a decision as to government policy has been taken, any statistical information used to provide an informed background to the taking of the decision is not to be regarded—

(a) for the purposes of subsection (1)(a), as relating to the formulation or development of government policy, or

(b) for the purposes of subsection (1)(b), as relating to Ministerial communications.

(3) The duty to confirm or deny does not arise in relation to information which is (or if it were held by the public authority would be) exempt information by virtue of subsection (1).

(4) In making any determination required by section 2(1)(b) or (2)(b) in relation to information which is exempt information by virtue of subsection (1)(a), regard shall be had to the particular public interest in the disclosure of factual information which has been used, or is intended to be used, to provide an informed background to decision-taking.

(5) In this section—

"government policy" includes the policy of the Executive Committee of the Northern Ireland Assembly and the policy of the National Assembly for Wales;

"the Law Officers" means the Attorney General, the Solicitor General, the Advocate General for Scotland, the Lord Advocate, the Solicitor General for Scotland and the Attorney General for Northern Ireland;

"Ministerial communications" means any communications—

(a) between Ministers of the Crown,

(b) between Northern Ireland Ministers, including Northern Ireland junior Ministers, or

(c) between Assembly Secretaries, including the Assembly First Secretary,

and includes, in particular, proceedings of the Cabinet or of any committee of the Cabinet, proceedings of the Executive Committee of the Northern Ireland Assembly, and proceedings of the executive committee of the National Assembly for Wales;

"Ministerial private office" means any part of a government department which provides personal administrative support to a Minister of the Crown, to a Northern Ireland Minister or a Northern Ireland junior Minister or any part of the administration of the National Assembly for Wales providing personal administrative support to the Assembly First Secretary or an Assembly Secretary;

"Northern Ireland junior Minister" means a member of the Northern Ireland Assembly appointed as a junior Minister under section 19 of the Northern Ireland Act 1998.

1998 c. 47.

36.—(1) This section applies to—

Prejudice to effective conduct of public affairs.

(a) information which is held by a government department or by the National Assembly for Wales and is not exempt information by virtue of section 35, and

(b) information which is held by any other public authority.

(2) Information to which this section applies is exempt information if, in the reasonable opinion of a qualified person, disclosure of the information under this Act—

    (a) would, or would be likely to, prejudice—

        (i) the maintenance of the convention of the collective responsibility of Ministers of the Crown, or

        (ii) the work of the Executive Committee of the Northern Ireland Assembly, or

        (iii) the work of the executive committee of the National Assembly for Wales,

    (b) would, or would be likely to, inhibit—

        (i) the free and frank provision of advice, or

        (ii) the free and frank exchange of views for the purposes of deliberation, or

    (c) would otherwise prejudice, or would be likely otherwise to prejudice, the effective conduct of public affairs.

(3) The duty to confirm or deny does not arise in relation to information to which this section applies (or would apply if held by the public authority) if, or to the extent that, in the reasonable opinion of a qualified person, compliance with section 1(1)(a) would, or would be likely to, have any of the effects mentioned in subsection (2).

(4) In relation to statistical information, subsections (2) and (3) shall have effect with the omission of the words "in the reasonable opinion of a qualified person".

(5) In subsections (2) and (3) "qualified person"—

    (a) in relation to information held by a government department in the charge of a Minister of the Crown, means any Minister of the Crown,

    (b) in relation to information held by a Northern Ireland department, means the Northern Ireland Minister in charge of the department,

    (c) in relation to information held by any other government department, means the commissioners or other person in charge of that department,

    (d) in relation to information held by the House of Commons, means the Speaker of that House,

    (e) in relation to information held by the House of Lords, means the Clerk of the Parliaments,

    (f) in relation to information held by the Northern Ireland Assembly, means the Presiding Officer,

    (g) in relation to information held by the National Assembly for Wales, means the Assembly First Secretary,

    (h) in relation to information held by any Welsh public authority other than the Auditor General for Wales, means—

        (i) the public authority, or

        (ii) any officer or employee of the authority authorised by the Assembly First Secretary,

    (i) in relation to information held by the National Audit Office, means the Comptroller and Auditor General,

(j) in relation to information held by the Northern Ireland Audit Office, means the Comptroller and Auditor General for Northern Ireland,

(k) in relation to information held by the Auditor General for Wales, means the Auditor General for Wales,

(l) in relation to information held by any Northern Ireland public authority other than the Northern Ireland Audit Office, means—

(i) the public authority, or

(ii) any officer or employee of the authority authorised by the First Minister and deputy First Minister in Northern Ireland acting jointly,

(m) in relation to information held by the Greater London Authority, means the Mayor of London,

(n) in relation to information held by a functional body within the meaning of the Greater London Authority Act 1999, means the chairman of that functional body, and

1999 c. 29.

(o) in relation to information held by any public authority not falling within any of paragraphs (a) to (n), means—

(i) a Minister of the Crown,

(ii) the public authority, if authorised for the purposes of this section by a Minister of the Crown, or

(iii) any officer or employee of the public authority who is authorised for the purposes of this section by a Minister of the Crown.

(6) Any authorisation for the purposes of this section—

(a) may relate to a specified person or to persons falling within a specified class,

(b) may be general or limited to particular classes of case, and

(c) may be granted subject to conditions.

(7) A certificate signed by the qualified person referred to in subsection (5)(d) or (e) above certifying that in his reasonable opinion—

(a) disclosure of information held by either House of Parliament, or

(b) compliance with section 1(1)(a) by either House,

would, or would be likely to, have any of the effects mentioned in subsection (2) shall be conclusive evidence of that fact.

37.—(1) Information is exempt information if it relates to—

Communications with Her Majesty, etc. and honours.

(a) communications with Her Majesty, with other members of the Royal Family or with the Royal Household, or

(b) the conferring by the Crown of any honour or dignity.

(2) The duty to confirm or deny does not arise in relation to information which is (or if it were held by the public authority would be) exempt information by virtue of subsection (1).

38.—(1) Information is exempt information if its disclosure under this Act would, or would be likely to—

Health and safety.

(a) endanger the physical or mental health of any individual, or

(b) endanger the safety of any individual.

(2) The duty to confirm or deny does not arise if, or to the extent that, compliance with section 1(1)(a) would, or would be likely to, have either of the effects mentioned in subsection (1).

Environmental
information.

39.—(1) Information is exempt information if the public authority holding it—

(a) is obliged by regulations under section 74 to make the information available to the public in accordance with the regulations, or

(b) would be so obliged but for any exemption contained in the regulations.

(2) The duty to confirm or deny does not arise in relation to information which is (or if it were held by the public authority would be) exempt information by virtue of subsection (1).

(3) Subsection (1)(a) does not limit the generality of section 21(1).

Personal
information.

40.—(1) Any information to which a request for information relates is exempt information if it constitutes personal data of which the applicant is the data subject.

(2) Any information to which a request for information relates is also exempt information if—

(a) it constitutes personal data which do not fall within subsection (1), and

(b) either the first or the second condition below is satisfied.

(3) The first condition is—

(a) in a case where the information falls within any of paragraphs (a) to (d) of the definition of "data" in section 1(1) of the Data Protection Act 1998, that the disclosure of the information to a member of the public otherwise than under this Act would contravene—

(i) any of the data protection principles, or

(ii) section 10 of that Act (right to prevent processing likely to cause damage or distress), and

1998 c. 29.

(b) in any other case, that the disclosure of the information to a member of the public otherwise than under this Act would contravene any of the data protection principles if the exemptions in section 33A(1) of the Data Protection Act 1998 (which relate to manual data held by public authorities) were disregarded.

(4) The second condition is that by virtue of any provision of Part IV of the Data Protection Act 1998 the information is exempt from section 7(1)(c) of that Act (data subject's right of access to personal data).

(5) The duty to confirm or deny—

(a) does not arise in relation to information which is (or if it were held by the public authority would be) exempt information by virtue of subsection (1), and

(b) does not arise in relation to other information if or to the extent that either—

(i) the giving to a member of the public of the confirmation or denial that would have to be given to comply with section 1(1)(a) would (apart from this Act) contravene any of the data protection principles or section 10 of the Data Protection Act 1998 or would do so if the exemptions in section 33A(1) of that Act were disregarded, or

1998 c. 29.

(ii) by virtue of any provision of Part IV of the Data Protection Act 1998 the information is exempt from section 7(1)(a) of that Act (data subject's right to be informed whether personal data being processed).

(6) In determining for the purposes of this section whether anything done before 24th October 2007 would contravene any of the data protection principles, the exemptions in Part III of Schedule 8 to the Data Protection Act 1998 shall be disregarded.

(7) In this section—

"the data protection principles" means the principles set out in Part I of Schedule 1 to the Data Protection Act 1998, as read subject to Part II of that Schedule and section 27(1) of that Act;

"data subject" has the same meaning as in section 1(1) of that Act;

"personal data" has the same meaning as in section 1(1) of that Act.

41.—(1) Information is exempt information if—

Information provided in confidence.

(a) it was obtained by the public authority from any other person (including another public authority), and

(b) the disclosure of the information to the public (otherwise than under this Act) by the public authority holding it would constitute a breach of confidence actionable by that or any other person.

(2) The duty to confirm or deny does not arise if, or to the extent that, the confirmation or denial that would have to be given to comply with section 1(1)(a) would (apart from this Act) constitute an actionable breach of confidence.

42.—(1) Information in respect of which a claim to legal professional privilege or, in Scotland, to confidentiality of communications could be maintained in legal proceedings is exempt information.

Legal professional privilege.

(2) The duty to confirm or deny does not arise if, or to the extent that, compliance with section 1(1)(a) would involve the disclosure of any information (whether or not already recorded) in respect of which such a claim could be maintained in legal proceedings.

43.—(1) Information is exempt information if it constitutes a trade secret.

Commercial interests.

(2) Information is exempt information if its disclosure under this Act would, or would be likely to, prejudice the commercial interests of any person (including the public authority holding it).

(3) The duty to confirm or deny does not arise if, or to the extent that, compliance with section 1(1)(a) would, or would be likely to, prejudice the interests mentioned in subsection (2).

44.—(1) Information is exempt information if its disclosure (otherwise than under this Act) by the public authority holding it—

(a) is prohibited by or under any enactment,

(b) is incompatible with any Community obligation, or

(c) would constitute or be punishable as a contempt of court.

(2) The duty to confirm or deny does not arise if the confirmation or denial that would have to be given to comply with section 1(1)(a) would (apart from this Act) fall within any of paragraphs (a) to (c) of subsection (1).

PART III

GENERAL FUNCTIONS OF SECRETARY OF STATE, LORD CHANCELLOR AND INFORMATION COMMISSIONER

45.—(1) The Secretary of State shall issue, and may from time to time revise, a code of practice providing guidance to public authorities as to the practice which it would, in his opinion, be desirable for them to follow in connection with the discharge of the authorities' functions under Part I.

(2) The code of practice must, in particular, include provision relating to—

(a) the provision of advice and assistance by public authorities to persons who propose to make, or have made, requests for information to them,

(b) the transfer of requests by one public authority to another public authority by which the information requested is or may be held,

(c) consultation with persons to whom the information requested relates or persons whose interests are likely to be affected by the disclosure of information,

(d) the inclusion in contracts entered into by public authorities of terms relating to the disclosure of information, and

(e) the provision by public authorities of procedures for dealing with complaints about the handling by them of requests for information.

(3) The code may make different provision for different public authorities.

(4) Before issuing or revising any code under this section, the Secretary of State shall consult the Commissioner.

(5) The Secretary of State shall lay before each House of Parliament any code or revised code made under this section.

Issue of code of
practice by Lord
Chancellor.

46.—(1) The Lord Chancellor shall issue, and may from time to time revise, a code of practice providing guidance to relevant authorities as to the practice which it would, in his opinion, be desirable for them to follow in connection with the keeping, management and destruction of their records.

(2) For the purpose of facilitating the performance by the Public Record Office, the Public Record Office of Northern Ireland and other public authorities of their functions under this Act in relation to records

which are public records for the purposes of the Public Records Act 1958 or the Public Records Act (Northern Ireland) 1923, the code may also include guidance as to—

(a) the practice to be adopted in relation to the transfer of records under section 3(4) of the Public Records Act 1958 or section 3 of the Public Records Act (Northern Ireland) 1923, and

(b) the practice of reviewing records before they are transferred under those provisions.

(3) In exercising his functions under this section, the Lord Chancellor shall have regard to the public interest in allowing public access to information held by relevant authorities.

(4) The code may make different provision for different relevant authorities.

(5) Before issuing or revising any code under this section the Lord Chancellor shall consult—

(a) the Secretary of State,

(b) the Commissioner, and

(c) in relation to Northern Ireland, the appropriate Northern Ireland Minister.

(6) The Lord Chancellor shall lay before each House of Parliament any code or revised code made under this section.

(7) In this section "relevant authority" means—

(a) any public authority, and

(b) any office or body which is not a public authority but whose administrative and departmental records are public records for the purposes of the Public Records Act 1958 or the Public Records Act (Northern Ireland) 1923.

47.—(1) It shall be the duty of the Commissioner to promote the following of good practice by public authorities and, in particular, so to perform his functions under this Act as to promote the observance by public authorities of—

General functions of Commissioner.

(a) the requirements of this Act, and

(b) the provisions of the codes of practice under sections 45 and 46.

(2) The Commissioner shall arrange for the dissemination in such form and manner as he considers appropriate of such information as it may appear to him expedient to give to the public—

(a) about the operation of this Act,

(b) about good practice, and

(c) about other matters within the scope of his functions under this Act,

and may give advice to any person as to any of those matters.

(3) The Commissioner may, with the consent of any public authority, assess whether that authority is following good practice.

(4) The Commissioner may charge such sums as he may with the consent of the Secretary of State determine for any services provided by the Commissioner under this section.

PART III

(5) The Commissioner shall from time to time as he considers appropriate—

(a) consult the Keeper of Public Records about the promotion by the Commissioner of the observance by public authorities of the provisions of the code of practice under section 46 in relation to records which are public records for the purposes of the Public Records Act 1958, and

1958 c. 51.

(b) consult the Deputy Keeper of the Records of Northern Ireland about the promotion by the Commissioner of the observance by public authorities of those provisions in relation to records which are public records for the purposes of the Public Records Act (Northern Ireland) 1923.

1923 c. 20 (N.I.).

(6) In this section "good practice", in relation to a public authority, means such practice in the discharge of its functions under this Act as appears to the Commissioner to be desirable, and includes (but is not limited to) compliance with the requirements of this Act and the provisions of the codes of practice under sections 45 and 46.

Recommendations as to good practice.

48.—(1) If it appears to the Commissioner that the practice of a public authority in relation to the exercise of its functions under this Act does not conform with that proposed in the codes of practice under sections 45 and 46, he may give to the authority a recommendation (in this section referred to as a "practice recommendation") specifying the steps which ought in his opinion to be taken for promoting such conformity.

(2) A practice recommendation must be given in writing and must refer to the particular provisions of the code of practice with which, in the Commissioner's opinion, the public authority's practice does not conform.

(3) Before giving to a public authority other than the Public Record Office a practice recommendation which relates to conformity with the code of practice under section 46 in respect of records which are public records for the purposes of the Public Records Act 1958, the Commissioner shall consult the Keeper of Public Records.

(4) Before giving to a public authority other than the Public Record Office of Northern Ireland a practice recommendation which relates to conformity with the code of practice under section 46 in respect of records which are public records for the purposes of the Public Records Act (Northern Ireland) 1923, the Commissioner shall consult the Deputy Keeper of the Records of Northern Ireland.

Reports to be laid before Parliament.

49.—(1) The Commissioner shall lay annually before each House of Parliament a general report on the exercise of his functions under this Act.

(2) The Commissioner may from time to time lay before each House of Parliament such other reports with respect to those functions as he thinks fit.

PART IV

ENFORCEMENT

50.—(1) Any person (in this section referred to as "the complainant") may apply to the Commissioner for a decision whether, in any specified respect, a request for information made by the complainant to a public authority has been dealt with in accordance with the requirements of Part I.

(2) On receiving an application under this section, the Commissioner shall make a decision unless it appears to him—

    (a) that the complainant has not exhausted any complaints procedure which is provided by the public authority in conformity with the code of practice under section 45,

    (b) that there has been undue delay in making the application,

    (c) that the application is frivolous or vexatious, or

    (d) that the application has been withdrawn or abandoned.

(3) Where the Commissioner has received an application under this section, he shall either—

    (a) notify the complainant that he has not made any decision under this section as a result of the application and of his grounds for not doing so, or

    (b) serve notice of his decision (in this Act referred to as a "decision notice") on the complainant and the public authority.

(4) Where the Commissioner decides that a public authority—

    (a) has failed to communicate information, or to provide confirmation or denial, in a case where it is required to do so by section 1(1), or

    (b) has failed to comply with any of the requirements of sections 11 and 17,

the decision notice must specify the steps which must be taken by the authority for complying with that requirement and the period within which they must be taken.

(5) A decision notice must contain particulars of the right of appeal conferred by section 57.

(6) Where a decision notice requires steps to be taken by the public authority within a specified period, the time specified in the notice must not expire before the end of the period within which an appeal can be brought against the notice and, if such an appeal is brought, no step which is affected by the appeal need be taken pending the determination or withdrawal of the appeal.

(7) This section has effect subject to section 53.

51.—(1) If the Commissioner—

    (a) has received an application under section 50, or

    (b) reasonably requires any information—

        (i) for the purpose of determining whether a public authority has complied or is complying with any of the requirements of Part I, or

Application for decision by Commissioner.

Information notices.

(ii) for the purpose of determining whether the practice of a public authority in relation to the exercise of its functions under this Act conforms with that proposed in the codes of practice under sections 45 and 46,

he may serve the authority with a notice (in this Act referred to as "an information notice") requiring it, within such time as is specified in the notice, to furnish the Commissioner, in such form as may be so specified, with such information relating to the application, to compliance with Part I or to conformity with the code of practice as is so specified.

(2) An information notice must contain—

(a) in a case falling within subsection (1)(a), a statement that the Commissioner has received an application under section 50, or

(b) in a case falling within subsection (1)(b), a statement—

(i) that the Commissioner regards the specified information as relevant for either of the purposes referred to in subsection (1)(b), and

(ii) of his reasons for regarding that information as relevant for that purpose.

(3) An information notice must also contain particulars of the right of appeal conferred by section 57.

(4) The time specified in an information notice must not expire before the end of the period within which an appeal can be brought against the notice and, if such an appeal is brought, the information need not be furnished pending the determination or withdrawal of the appeal.

(5) An authority shall not be required by virtue of this section to furnish the Commissioner with any information in respect of—

(a) any communication between a professional legal adviser and his client in connection with the giving of legal advice to the client with respect to his obligations, liabilities or rights under this Act, or

(b) any communication between a professional legal adviser and his client, or between such an adviser or his client and any other person, made in connection with or in contemplation of proceedings under or arising out of this Act (including proceedings before the Tribunal) and for the purposes of such proceedings.

(6) In subsection (5) references to the client of a professional legal adviser include references to any person representing such a client.

(7) The Commissioner may cancel an information notice by written notice to the authority on which it was served.

(8) In this section "information" includes unrecorded information.

Enforcement notices.

52.—(1) If the Commissioner is satisfied that a public authority has failed to comply with any of the requirements of Part I, the Commissioner may serve the authority with a notice (in this Act referred to as "an enforcement notice") requiring the authority to take, within such time as may be specified in the notice, such steps as may be so specified for complying with those requirements.

(2) An enforcement notice must contain—

(a) a statement of the requirement or requirements of Part I with which the Commissioner is satisfied that the public authority has failed to comply and his reasons for reaching that conclusion, and

(b) particulars of the right of appeal conferred by section 57.

(3) An enforcement notice must not require any of the provisions of the notice to be complied with before the end of the period within which an appeal can be brought against the notice and, if such an appeal is brought, the notice need not be complied with pending the determination or withdrawal of the appeal.

(4) The Commissioner may cancel an enforcement notice by written notice to the authority on which it was served.

(5) This section has effect subject to section 53.

53.—(1) This section applies to a decision notice or enforcement notice which—

> Exception from duty to comply with decision notice or enforcement notice.

(a) is served on—

> (i) a government department,
>
> (ii) the National Assembly for Wales, or
>
> (iii) any public authority designated for the purposes of this section by an order made by the Secretary of State, and

(b) relates to a failure, in respect of one or more requests for information—

> (i) to comply with section 1(1)(a) in respect of information which falls within any provision of Part II stating that the duty to confirm or deny does not arise, or
>
> (ii) to comply with section 1(1)(b) in respect of exempt information.

(2) A decision notice or enforcement notice to which this section applies shall cease to have effect if, not later than the twentieth working day following the effective date, the accountable person in relation to that authority gives the Commissioner a certificate signed by him stating that he has on reasonable grounds formed the opinion that, in respect of the request or requests concerned, there was no failure falling within subsection (1)(b).

(3) Where the accountable person gives a certificate to the Commissioner under subsection (2) he shall as soon as practicable thereafter lay a copy of the certificate before—

(a) each House of Parliament,

(b) the Northern Ireland Assembly, in any case where the certificate relates to a decision notice or enforcement notice which has been served on a Northern Ireland department or any Northern Ireland public authority, or

(c) the National Assembly for Wales, in any case where the certificate relates to a decision notice or enforcement notice which has been served on the National Assembly for Wales or any Welsh public authority.

(4) In subsection (2) "the effective date", in relation to a decision notice or enforcement notice, means—

(a) the day on which the notice was given to the public authority, or

(b) where an appeal under section 57 is brought, the day on which that appeal (or any further appeal arising out of it) is determined or withdrawn.

(5) Before making an order under subsection (1)(a)(iii), the Secretary of State shall—

(a) if the order relates to a Welsh public authority, consult the National Assembly for Wales,

(b) if the order relates to the Northern Ireland Assembly, consult the Presiding Officer of that Assembly, and

(c) if the order relates to a Northern Ireland public authority, consult the First Minister and deputy First Minister in Northern Ireland.

(6) Where the accountable person gives a certificate to the Commissioner under subsection (2) in relation to a decision notice, the accountable person shall, on doing so or as soon as reasonably practicable after doing so, inform the person who is the complainant for the purposes of section 50 of the reasons for his opinion.

(7) The accountable person is not obliged to provide information under subsection (6) if, or to the extent that, compliance with that subsection would involve the disclosure of exempt information.

(8) In this section "the accountable person"—

(a) in relation to a Northern Ireland department or any Northern Ireland public authority, means the First Minister and deputy First Minister in Northern Ireland acting jointly,

(b) in relation to the National Assembly for Wales or any Welsh public authority, means the Assembly First Secretary, and

(c) in relation to any other public authority, means—

(i) a Minister of the Crown who is a member of the Cabinet, or

(ii) the Attorney General, the Advocate General for Scotland or the Attorney General for Northern Ireland.

(9) In this section "working day" has the same meaning as in section 10.

Failure to comply with notice.   **54.**—(1) If a public authority has failed to comply with—

(a) so much of a decision notice as requires steps to be taken,

(b) an information notice, or

(c) an enforcement notice,

the Commissioner may certify in writing to the court that the public authority has failed to comply with that notice.

(2) For the purposes of this section, a public authority which, in purported compliance with an information notice—

(a) makes a statement which it knows to be false in a material respect, or

(b) recklessly makes a statement which is false in a material respect,

is to be taken to have failed to comply with the notice.

(3) Where a failure to comply is certified under subsection (1), the court may inquire into the matter and, after hearing any witness who may be produced against or on behalf of the public authority, and after hearing any statement that may be offered in defence, deal with the authority as if it had committed a contempt of court.

(4) In this section "the court" means the High Court or, in Scotland, the Court of Session.

55. Schedule 3 (powers of entry and inspection) has effect.

Powers of entry and inspection.

56.—(1) This Act does not confer any right of action in civil proceedings in respect of any failure to comply with any duty imposed by or under this Act.

No action against public authority.

(2) Subsection (1) does not affect the powers of the Commissioner under section 54.

PART V

APPEALS

57.—(1) Where a decision notice has been served, the complainant or the public authority may appeal to the Tribunal against the notice.

Appeal against notices served under Part IV.

(2) A public authority on which an information notice or an enforcement notice has been served by the Commissioner may appeal to the Tribunal against the notice.

(3) In relation to a decision notice or enforcement notice which relates—

    (a) to information to which section 66 applies, and

    (b) to a matter which by virtue of subsection (3) or (4) of that section falls to be determined by the responsible authority instead of the appropriate records authority,

subsections (1) and (2) shall have effect as if the reference to the public authority were a reference to the public authority or the responsible authority.

58.—(1) If on an appeal under section 57 the Tribunal considers—

Determination of appeals.

    (a) that the notice against which the appeal is brought is not in accordance with the law, or

    (b) to the extent that the notice involved an exercise of discretion by the Commissioner, that he ought to have exercised his discretion differently,

the Tribunal shall allow the appeal or substitute such other notice as could have been served by the Commissioner; and in any other case the Tribunal shall dismiss the appeal.

(2) On such an appeal, the Tribunal may review any finding of fact on which the notice in question was based.

59. Any party to an appeal to the Tribunal under section 57 may appeal from the decision of the Tribunal on a point of law to the appropriate court; and that court shall be—

Appeals from decision of Tribunal.

  (a) the High Court of Justice in England if the address of the public authority is in England or Wales,

  (b) the Court of Session if that address is in Scotland, and

  (c) the High Court of Justice in Northern Ireland if that address is in Northern Ireland.

Appeals against national security certificate.

60.—(1) Where a certificate under section 23(2) or 24(3) has been issued—

  (a) the Commissioner, or

  (b) any applicant whose request for information is affected by the issue of the certificate,

may appeal to the Tribunal against the certificate.

  (2) If on an appeal under subsection (1) relating to a certificate under section 23(2), the Tribunal finds that the information referred to in the certificate was not exempt information by virtue of section 23(1), the Tribunal may allow the appeal and quash the certificate.

  (3) If on an appeal under subsection (1) relating to a certificate under section 24(3), the Tribunal finds that, applying the principles applied by the court on an application for judicial review, the Minister did not have reasonable grounds for issuing the certificate, the Tribunal may allow the appeal and quash the certificate.

  (4) Where in any proceedings under this Act it is claimed by a public authority that a certificate under section 24(3) which identifies the information to which it applies by means of a general description applies to particular information, any other party to the proceedings may appeal to the Tribunal on the ground that the certificate does not apply to the information in question and, subject to any determination under subsection (5), the certificate shall be conclusively presumed so to apply.

  (5) On any appeal under subsection (4), the Tribunal may determine that the certificate does not so apply.

Appeal proceedings.
1998 c. 29.

61.—(1) Schedule 4 (which contains amendments of Schedule 6 to the Data Protection Act 1998 relating to appeal proceedings) has effect.

  (2) Accordingly, the provisions of Schedule 6 to the Data Protection Act 1998 have effect (so far as applicable) in relation to appeals under this Part.

PART VI

HISTORICAL RECORDS AND RECORDS IN PUBLIC RECORD OFFICE OR PUBLIC RECORD OFFICE OF NORTHERN IRELAND

Interpretation of Part VI.

62.—(1) For the purposes of this Part, a record becomes a "historical record" at the end of the period of thirty years beginning with the year following that in which it was created.

  (2) Where records created at different dates are for administrative purposes kept together in one file or other assembly, all the records in that file or other assembly are to be treated for the purposes of this Part as having been created when the latest of those records was created.

  (3) In this Part "year" means a calendar year.

63.—(1) Information contained in a historical record cannot be exempt information by virtue of section 28, 30(1), 32, 33, 35, 36, 37(1)(a), 42 or 43.

Removal of exemptions: historical records generally.

(2) Compliance with section 1(1)(a) in relation to a historical record is not to be taken to be capable of having any of the effects referred to in section 28(3), 33(3), 36(3), 42(2) or 43(3).

(3) Information cannot be exempt information by virtue of section 37(1)(b) after the end of the period of sixty years beginning with the year following that in which the record containing the information was created.

(4) Information cannot be exempt information by virtue of section 31 after the end of the period of one hundred years beginning with the year following that in which the record containing the information was created.

(5) Compliance with section 1(1)(a) in relation to any record is not to be taken, at any time after the end of the period of one hundred years beginning with the year following that in which the record was created, to be capable of prejudicing any of the matters referred to in section 31(1).

64.—(1) Information contained in a historical record in the Public Record Office or the Public Record Office of Northern Ireland cannot be exempt information by virtue of section 21 or 22.

Removal of exemptions: historical records in public record offices.

(2) In relation to any information falling within section 23(1) which is contained in a historical record in the Public Record Office or the Public Record Office of Northern Ireland, section 2(3) shall have effect with the omission of the reference to section 23.

65.—(1) Before refusing a request for information relating to information which is contained in a historical record and is exempt information only by virtue of a provision not specified in section 2(3), a public authority shall—

Decisions as to refusal of discretionary disclosure of historical records.

(a) if the historical record is a public record within the meaning of the Public Records Act 1958, consult the Lord Chancellor, or

1958 c. 51.

(b) if the historical record is a public record to which the Public Records Act (Northern Ireland) 1923 applies, consult the appropriate Northern Ireland Minister.

1923 c. 20 (N.I.).

(2) This section does not apply to information to which section 66 applies.

66.—(1) This section applies to any information which is (or, if it existed, would be) contained in a transferred public record, other than information which the responsible authority has designated as open information for the purposes of this section.

Decisions relating to certain transferred public records.

(2) Before determining whether—

(a) information to which this section applies falls within any provision of Part II relating to the duty to confirm or deny, or

(b) information to which this section applies is exempt information,

the appropriate records authority shall consult the responsible authority.

(3) Where information to which this section applies falls within a provision of Part II relating to the duty to confirm or deny but does not fall within any of the provisions of that Part relating to that duty which

are specified in subsection (3) of section 2, any question as to the application of subsection (1)(b) of that section is to be determined by the responsible authority instead of the appropriate records authority.

(4) Where any information to which this section applies is exempt information only by virtue of any provision of Part II not specified in subsection (3) of section 2, any question as to the application of subsection (2)(b) of that section is to be determined by the responsible authority instead of the appropriate records authority.

(5) Before making by virtue of subsection (3) or (4) any determination that subsection (1)(b) or (2)(b) of section 2 applies, the responsible authority shall consult—

1958 c. 51.

(a) where the transferred public record is a public record within the meaning of the Public Records Act 1958, the Lord Chancellor, and

1923 c. 20 (N.I.).

(b) where the transferred public record is a public record to which the Public Records Act (Northern Ireland) 1923 applies, the appropriate Northern Ireland Minister.

(6) Where the responsible authority in relation to information to which this section applies is not (apart from this subsection) a public authority, it shall be treated as being a public authority for the purposes of Parts III, IV and V of this Act so far as relating to—

(a) the duty imposed by section 15(3), and

(b) the imposition of any requirement to furnish information relating to compliance with Part I in connection with the information to which this section applies.

Amendments of public records legislation.

67. Schedule 5 (which amends the Public Records Act 1958 and the Public Records Act (Northern Ireland) 1923) has effect.

Part VII

Amendments of Data Protection Act 1998

Amendments relating to personal information held by public authorities

Extension of meaning of "data".
1998 c. 29.

68.—(1) Section 1 of the Data Protection Act 1998 (basic interpretative provisions) is amended in accordance with subsections (2) and (3).

(2) In subsection (1)—

(a) in the definition of "data", the word "or" at the end of paragraph (c) is omitted and after paragraph (d) there is inserted "or

(e) is recorded information held by a public authority and does not fall within any of paragraphs (a) to (d);", and

(b) after the definition of "processing" there is inserted—

""public authority" has the same meaning as in the Freedom of Information Act 2000;".

(3) After subsection (4) there is inserted—

"(5) In paragraph (e) of the definition of "data" in subsection (1), the reference to information "held" by a public authority shall be construed in accordance with section 3(2) of the Freedom of Information Act 2000.

(6) Where section 7 of the Freedom of Information Act 2000 prevents Parts I to V of that Act from applying to certain information held by a public authority, that information is not to be treated for the purposes of paragraph (e) of the definition of "data" in subsection (1) as held by a public authority."

(4) In section 56 of that Act (prohibition of requirement as to production of certain records), after subsection (6) there is inserted—

"(6A) A record is not a relevant record to the extent that it relates, or is to relate, only to personal data falling within paragraph (e) of the definition of "data" in section 1(1)."

(5) In the Table in section 71 of that Act (index of defined expressions) after the entry relating to processing there is inserted—

"public authority   section 1(1)".

69.—(1) In section 7(1) of the Data Protection Act 1998 (right of access to personal data), for "sections 8 and 9" there is substituted "sections 8, 9 and 9A".

Right of access to unstructured personal data held by public authorities.
1998 c. 29.

(2) After section 9 of that Act there is inserted—

"Unstructured personal data held by public authorities.

9A.—(1) In this section "unstructured personal data" means any personal data falling within paragraph (e) of the definition of "data" in section 1(1), other than information which is recorded as part of, or with the intention that it should form part of, any set of information relating to individuals to the extent that the set is structured by reference to individuals or by reference to criteria relating to individuals.

(2) A public authority is not obliged to comply with subsection (1) of section 7 in relation to any unstructured personal data unless the request under that section contains a description of the data.

(3) Even if the data are described by the data subject in his request, a public authority is not obliged to comply with subsection (1) of section 7 in relation to unstructured personal data if the authority estimates that the cost of complying with the request so far as relating to those data would exceed the appropriate limit.

(4) Subsection (3) does not exempt the public authority from its obligation to comply with paragraph (a) of section 7(1) in relation to the unstructured personal data unless the estimated cost of complying with that paragraph alone in relation to those data would exceed the appropriate limit.

(5) In subsections (3) and (4) "the appropriate limit" means such amount as may be prescribed by the Secretary of State by regulations, and different amounts may be prescribed in relation to different cases.

(6) Any estimate for the purposes of this section must be made in accordance with regulations under section 12(5) of the Freedom of Information Act 2000."

(3) In section 67(5) of that Act (statutory instruments subject to negative resolution procedure), in paragraph (c), for "or 9(3)" there is substituted ", 9(3) or 9A(5)".

Exemptions applicable to certain manual data held by public authorities. 1998 c. 29.

70.—(1) After section 33 of the Data Protection Act 1998 there is inserted—

"Manual data held by public authorities.

33A.—(1) Personal data falling within paragraph (e) of the definition of "data" in section 1(1) are exempt from—

    (a) the first, second, third, fifth, seventh and eighth data protection principles,

    (b) the sixth data protection principle except so far as it relates to the rights conferred on data subjects by sections 7 and 14,

    (c) sections 10 to 12,

    (d) section 13, except so far as it relates to damage caused by a contravention of section 7 or of the fourth data protection principle and to any distress which is also suffered by reason of that contravention,

    (e) Part III, and

    (f) section 55.

(2) Personal data which fall within paragraph (e) of the definition of "data" in section 1(1) and relate to appointments or removals, pay, discipline, superannuation or other personnel matters, in relation to—

    (a) service in any of the armed forces of the Crown,

    (b) service in any office or employment under the Crown or under any public authority, or

    (c) service in any office or employment, or under any contract for services, in respect of which power to take action, or to determine or approve the action taken, in such matters is vested in Her Majesty, any Minister of the Crown, the National Assembly for Wales, any Northern Ireland Minister (within the meaning of the Freedom of Information Act 2000) or any public authority,

are also exempt from the remaining data protection principles and the remaining provisions of Part II."

(2) In section 55 of that Act (unlawful obtaining etc. of personal data) in subsection (8) after "section 28" there is inserted "or 33A".

(3) In Part III of Schedule 8 to that Act (exemptions available after 23rd October 2001 but before 24th October 2007) after paragraph 14 there is inserted—

"14A.—(1) This paragraph applies to personal data which fall within paragraph (e) of the definition of "data" in section 1(1) and do not fall within paragraph 14(1)(a), but does not apply to eligible manual data to which the exemption in paragraph 16 applies.

(2) During the second transitional period, data to which this paragraph applies are exempt from—

    (a) the fourth data protection principle, and

    (b) section 14(1) to (3)."

(4) In Schedule 13 to that Act (modifications of Act having effect before 24th October 2007) in subsection (4)(b) of section 12A to that Act as set out in paragraph 1, after "paragraph 14" there is inserted "or 14A".

71. In section 16(1) of the Data Protection Act 1998 (the registrable particulars), before the word "and" at the end of paragraph (f) there is inserted—

    "(ff) where the data controller is a public authority, a statement of that fact,".

Particulars registrable under Part III of Data Protection Act 1998.

1998 c. 29.

72. In section 34 of the Data Protection Act 1998 (information available to the public by or under enactment), after the word "enactment" there is inserted "other than an enactment contained in the Freedom of Information Act 2000".

Availability under Act disregarded for purpose of exemption.

Other amendments

73. Schedule 6 (which contains further amendments of the Data Protection Act 1998) has effect.

Further amendments of Data Protection Act 1998.

PART VIII

MISCELLANEOUS AND SUPPLEMENTAL

74.—(1) In this section "the Aarhus Convention" means the Convention on Access to Information, Public Participation in Decision-making and Access to Justice in Environmental Matters signed at Aarhus on 25th June 1998.

Power to make provision relating to environmental information.

(2) For the purposes of this section "the information provisions" of the Aarhus Convention are Article 4, together with Articles 3 and 9 so far as relating to that Article.

(3) The Secretary of State may by regulations make such provision as he considers appropriate—

    (a) for the purpose of implementing the information provisions of the Aarhus Convention or any amendment of those provisions made in accordance with Article 14 of the Convention, and

    (b) for the purpose of dealing with matters arising out of or related to the implementation of those provisions or of any such amendment.

(4) Regulations under subsection (3) may in particular—

    (a) enable charges to be made for making information available in accordance with the regulations,

    (b) provide that any obligation imposed by the regulations in relation to the disclosure of information is to have effect notwithstanding any enactment or rule of law,

    (c) make provision for the issue by the Secretary of State of a code of practice,

      (d) provide for sections 47 and 48 to apply in relation to such a code with such modifications as may be specified,

      (e) provide for any of the provisions of Parts IV and V to apply, with such modifications as may be specified in the regulations, in relation to compliance with any requirement of the regulations, and

      (f) contain such transitional or consequential provision (including provision modifying any enactment) as the Secretary of State considers appropriate.

  (5) This section has effect subject to section 80.

Power to amend or repeal enactments prohibiting disclosure of information.

75.—(1) If, with respect to any enactment which prohibits the disclosure of information held by a public authority, it appears to the Secretary of State that by virtue of section 44(1)(a) the enactment is capable of preventing the disclosure of information under section 1, he may by order repeal or amend the enactment for the purpose of removing or relaxing the prohibition.

  (2) In subsection (1)—

"enactment" means—

      (a) any enactment contained in an Act passed before or in the same Session as this Act, or

      (b) any enactment contained in Northern Ireland legislation or subordinate legislation passed or made before the passing of this Act;

"information" includes unrecorded information.

  (3) An order under this section may do all or any of the following—

      (a) make such modifications of enactments as, in the opinion of the Secretary of State, are consequential upon, or incidental to, the amendment or repeal of the enactment containing the prohibition;

      (b) contain such transitional provisions and savings as appear to the Secretary of State to be appropriate;

      (c) make different provision for different cases.

Disclosure of information between Commissioner and ombudsmen. 1998 c. 29.

76.—(1) The Commissioner may disclose to a person specified in the first column of the Table below any information obtained by, or furnished to, the Commissioner under or for the purposes of this Act or the Data Protection Act 1998 if it appears to the Commissioner that the information relates to a matter which could be the subject of an investigation by that person under the enactment specified in relation to that person in the second column of that Table.

TABLE

Ombudsman	*Enactment*
The Parliamentary Commissioner for Administration.	The Parliamentary Commissioner Act 1967 (c. 13).
The Health Service Commissioner for England.	The Health Service Commissioners Act 1993 (c. 46).
The Health Service Commissioner for Wales.	The Health Service Commissioners Act 1993 (c. 46).
The Health Service Commissioner for Scotland.	The Health Service Commissioners Act 1993 (c. 46).
A Local Commissioner as defined by section 23(3) of the Local Government Act 1974.	Part III of the Local Government Act 1974 (c. 7).
The Commissioner for Local Administration in Scotland.	Part II of the Local Government (Scotland) Act 1975 (c. 30).
The Scottish Parliamentary Commissioner for Administration.	The Scotland Act 1998 (Transitory and Transitional Provisions)(Complaints of Maladministration) Order 1999 (S.I. 1999/1351).
The Welsh Administration Ombudsman.	Schedule 9 to the Government of Wales Act 1998 (c. 38).
The Northern Ireland Commissioner for Complaints.	The Commissioner for Complaints (Northern Ireland) Order 1996 (S.I. 1996/1297 (N.I. 7)).
The Assembly Ombudsman for Northern Ireland.	The Ombudsman (Northern Ireland) Order 1996 (S.I. 1996/1298 (N.I. 8)).

(2) Schedule 7 (which contains amendments relating to information disclosed to ombudsmen under subsection (1) and to the disclosure of information by ombudsmen to the Commissioner) has effect.

77.—(1) Where—

    (a) a request for information has been made to a public authority, and

Offence of altering etc. records with intent to prevent disclosure.

PART VIII
1988 c. 29.

(b) under section 1 of this Act or section 7 of the Data Protection Act 1998, the applicant would have been entitled (subject to payment of any fee) to communication of any information in accordance with that section,

any person to whom this subsection applies is guilty of an offence if he alters, defaces, blocks, erases, destroys or conceals any record held by the public authority, with the intention of preventing the disclosure by that authority of all, or any part, of the information to the communication of which the applicant would have been entitled.

(2) Subsection (1) applies to the public authority and to any person who is employed by, is an officer of, or is subject to the direction of, the public authority.

(3) A person guilty of an offence under this section is liable on summary conviction to a fine not exceeding level 5 on the standard scale.

(4) No proceedings for an offence under this section shall be instituted—

(a) in England or Wales, except by the Commissioner or by or with the consent of the Director of Public Prosecutions;

(b) in Northern Ireland, except by the Commissioner or by or with the consent of the Director of Public Prosecutions for Northern Ireland.

Saving for existing powers.

78. Nothing in this Act is to be taken to limit the powers of a public authority to disclose information held by it.

Defamation.

79. Where any information communicated by a public authority to a person ("the applicant") under section 1 was supplied to the public authority by a third person, the publication to the applicant of any defamatory matter contained in the information shall be privileged unless the publication is shown to have been made with malice.

Scotland.

80.—(1) No order may be made under section 4(1) or 5 in relation to any of the bodies specified in subsection (2); and the power conferred by section 74(3) does not include power to make provision in relation to information held by any of those bodies.

(2) The bodies referred to in subsection (1) are—

(a) the Scottish Parliament,

(b) any part of the Scottish Administration,

(c) the Scottish Parliamentary Corporate Body, or

1998 c. 46.

(d) any Scottish public authority with mixed functions or no reserved functions (within the meaning of the Scotland Act 1998).

Application to government departments, etc.

81.—(1) For the purposes of this Act each government department is to be treated as a person separate from any other government department.

(2) Subsection (1) does not enable—

(a) a government department which is not a Northern Ireland department to claim for the purposes of section 41(1)(b) that the disclosure of any information by it would constitute a breach of confidence actionable by any other government department (not being a Northern Ireland department), or

(b) a Northern Ireland department to claim for those purposes that the disclosure of information by it would constitute a breach of confidence actionable by any other Northern Ireland department.

(3) A government department is not liable to prosecution under this Act, but section 77 and paragraph 12 of Schedule 3 apply to a person in the public service of the Crown as they apply to any other person.

(4) The provisions specified in subsection (3) also apply to a person acting on behalf of either House of Parliament or on behalf of the Northern Ireland Assembly as they apply to any other person.

82.—(1) Any power of the Secretary of State to make an order or regulations under this Act shall be exercisable by statutory instrument.

Orders and regulations.

(2) A statutory instrument containing (whether alone or with other provisions)—

(a) an order under section 5, 7(3) or (8), 53(1)(a)(iii) or 75, or

(b) regulations under section 10(4) or 74(3),

shall not be made unless a draft of the instrument has been laid before, and approved by a resolution of, each House of Parliament.

(3) A statutory instrument which contains (whether alone or with other provisions)—

(a) an order under section 4(1), or

(b) regulations under any provision of this Act not specified in subsection (2)(b),

and which is not subject to the requirement in subsection (2) that a draft of the instrument be laid before and approved by a resolution of each House of Parliament, shall be subject to annulment in pursuance of a resolution of either House of Parliament.

(4) An order under section 4(5) shall be laid before Parliament after being made.

(5) If a draft of an order under section 5 or 7(8) would, apart from this subsection, be treated for the purposes of the Standing Orders of either House of Parliament as a hybrid instrument, it shall proceed in that House as if it were not such an instrument.

83.—(1) In this Act "Welsh public authority" means—

Meaning of "Welsh public authority".

(a) any public authority which is listed in Part II, III, IV or VI of Schedule 1 and whose functions are exercisable only or mainly in or as regards Wales, other than an excluded authority, or

(b) any public authority which is an Assembly subsidiary as defined by section 99(4) of the Government of Wales Act 1998.

1998 c. 38.

(2) In paragraph (a) of subsection (1) "excluded authority" means a public authority which is designated by the Secretary of State by order as an excluded authority for the purposes of that paragraph.

(3) Before making an order under subsection (2), the Secretary of State shall consult the National Assembly for Wales.

Interpretation.

84. In this Act, unless the context otherwise requires—

"applicant", in relation to a request for information, means the person who made the request;

"appropriate Northern Ireland Minister" means the Northern Ireland Minister in charge of the Department of Culture, Arts and Leisure in Northern Ireland;

"appropriate records authority", in relation to a transferred public record, has the meaning given by section 15(5);

"body" includes an unincorporated association;

"the Commissioner" means the Information Commissioner;

"decision notice" has the meaning given by section 50;

"the duty to confirm or deny" has the meaning given by section 1(6);

"enactment" includes an enactment contained in Northern Ireland legislation;

"enforcement notice" has the meaning given by section 52;

"executive committee", in relation to the National Assembly for Wales, has the same meaning as in the Government of Wales Act 1998;

1998 c. 38.

"exempt information" means information which is exempt information by virtue of any provision of Part II;

"fees notice" has the meaning given by section 9(1);

"government department" includes a Northern Ireland department, the Northern Ireland Court Service and any other body or authority exercising statutory functions on behalf of the Crown, but does not include—

(a) any of the bodies specified in section 80(2),

(b) the Security Service, the Secret Intelligence Service or the Government Communications Headquarters, or

(c) the National Assembly for Wales;

"information" (subject to sections 51(8) and 75(2)) means information recorded in any form;

"information notice" has the meaning given by section 51;

"Minister of the Crown" has the same meaning as in the Ministers of the Crown Act 1975;

1975 c. 26.

"Northern Ireland Minister" includes the First Minister and deputy First Minister in Northern Ireland;

"Northern Ireland public authority" means any public authority, other than the Northern Ireland Assembly or a Northern Ireland department, whose functions are exercisable only or mainly in or as regards Northern Ireland and relate only or mainly to transferred matters;

"prescribed" means prescribed by regulations made by the Secretary of State;

"public authority" has the meaning given by section 3(1);

"public record" means a public record within the meaning of the Public Records Act 1958 or a public record to which the Public Records Act (Northern Ireland) 1923 applies; 1958 c. 51.
1923 c. 20 (N.I.).

"publication scheme" has the meaning given by section 19;

"request for information" has the meaning given by section 8;

"responsible authority", in relation to a transferred public record, has the meaning given by section 15(5);

"the special forces" means those units of the armed forces of the Crown the maintenance of whose capabilities is the responsibility of the Director of Special Forces or which are for the time being subject to the operational command of that Director;

"subordinate legislation" has the meaning given by subsection (1) of section 21 of the Interpretation Act 1978, except that the definition of that term in that subsection shall have effect as if "Act" included Northern Ireland legislation; 1978 c. 30.

"transferred matter", in relation to Northern Ireland, has the meaning given by section 4(1) of the Northern Ireland Act 1998; 1998 c. 47.

"transferred public record" has the meaning given by section 15(4);

"the Tribunal" means the Information Tribunal;

"Welsh public authority" has the meaning given by section 83.

85. There shall be paid out of money provided by Parliament— Expenses.

(a) any increase attributable to this Act in the expenses of the Secretary of State in respect of the Commissioner, the Tribunal or the members of the Tribunal,

(b) any administrative expenses of the Secretary of State attributable to this Act,

(c) any other expenses incurred in consequence of this Act by a Minister of the Crown or government department or by either House of Parliament, and

(d) any increase attributable to this Act in the sums which under any other Act are payable out of money so provided.

86. Schedule 8 (repeals) has effect. Repeals.

87.—(1) The following provisions of this Act shall come into force on the day on which this Act is passed— Commencement.

(a) sections 3 to 8 and Schedule 1,

(b) section 19 so far as relating to the approval of publication schemes,

(c) section 20 so far as relating to the approval and preparation by the Commissioner of model publication schemes,

(d) section 47(2) to (6),

(e) section 49,

(f) section 74,

(g) section 75,

(h) sections 78 to 85 and this section,

    (i) paragraphs 2 and 17 to 22 of Schedule 2 (and section 18(4) so far as relating to those paragraphs),

    (j) paragraph 4 of Schedule 5 (and section 67 so far as relating to that paragraph),

    (k) paragraph 8 of Schedule 6 (and section 73 so far as relating to that paragraph),

    (l) Part I of Schedule 8 (and section 86 so far as relating to that Part), and

    (m) so much of any other provision of this Act as confers power to make any order, regulations or code of practice.

(2) The following provisions of this Act shall come into force at the end of the period of two months beginning with the day on which this Act is passed—

    (a) section 18(1),

    (b) section 76 and Schedule 7,

    (c) paragraphs 1(1), 3(1), 4, 6, 7, 8(2), 9(2), 10(a), 13(1) and (2), 14(a) and 15(1) and (2) of Schedule 2 (and section 18(4) so far as relating to those provisions), and

    (d) Part II of Schedule 8 (and section 86 so far as relating to that Part).

(3) Except as provided by subsections (1) and (2), this Act shall come into force at the end of the period of five years beginning with the day on which this Act is passed or on such day before the end of that period as the Secretary of State may by order appoint; and different days may be appointed for different purposes.

(4) An order under subsection (3) may contain such transitional provisions and savings (including provisions capable of having effect after the end of the period referred to in that subsection) as the Secretary of State considers appropriate.

(5) During the twelve months beginning with the day on which this Act is passed, and during each subsequent complete period of twelve months in the period beginning with that day and ending with the first day on which all the provisions of this Act are fully in force, the Secretary of State shall—

    (a) prepare a report on his proposals for bringing fully into force those provisions of this Act which are not yet fully in force, and

    (b) lay a copy of the report before each House of Parliament.

Short title and extent.

88.—(1) This Act may be cited as the Freedom of Information Act 2000.

(2) Subject to subsection (3), this Act extends to Northern Ireland.

(3) The amendment or repeal of any enactment by this Act has the same extent as that enactment.

SCHEDULES

SCHEDULE 1

PUBLIC AUTHORITIES

PART I

GENERAL

1. Any government department.

2. The House of Commons.

3. The House of Lords.

4. The Northern Ireland Assembly.

5. The National Assembly for Wales.

6. The armed forces of the Crown, except—

    (a) the special forces, and

    (b) any unit or part of a unit which is for the time being required by the Secretary of State to assist the Government Communications Headquarters in the exercise of its functions.

PART II

LOCAL GOVERNMENT

England and Wales

7. A local authority within the meaning of the Local Government Act 1972, namely— 1972 c. 70.

    (a) in England, a county council, a London borough council, a district council or a parish council,

    (b) in Wales, a county council, a county borough council or a community council.

8. The Greater London Authority.

9. The Common Council of the City of London, in respect of information held in its capacity as a local authority, police authority or port health authority.

10. The Sub-Treasurer of the Inner Temple or the Under-Treasurer of the Middle Temple, in respect of information held in his capacity as a local authority.

11. The Council of the Isles of Scilly.

12. A parish meeting constituted under section 13 of the Local Government Act 1972.

13. Any charter trustees constituted under section 246 of the Local Government Act 1972.

14. A fire authority constituted by a combination scheme under section 5 or 6 of the Fire Services Act 1947. 1947 c. 41.

1985 c. 51.

15. A waste disposal authority established by virtue of an order under section 10(1) of the Local Government Act 1985.

1984 c. 22.

16. A port health authority constituted by an order under section 2 of the Public Health (Control of Disease) Act 1984.

1964 c. 26.

17. A licensing planning committee constituted under section 119 of the Licensing Act 1964.

1991 c. 59.

18. An internal drainage board which is continued in being by virtue of section 1 of the Land Drainage Act 1991.

19. A joint authority established under Part IV of the Local Government Act 1985 (fire services, civil defence and transport).

20. The London Fire and Emergency Planning Authority.

21. A joint fire authority established by virtue of an order under section 42(2) of the Local Government Act 1985 (reorganisation of functions).

22. A body corporate established pursuant to an order under section 67 of the Local Government Act 1985 (transfer of functions to successors of residuary bodies, etc.).

1992 c. 19.

23. A body corporate established pursuant to an order under section 22 of the Local Government Act 1992 (residuary bodies).

1988 c. 4.

24. The Broads Authority established by section 1 of the Norfolk and Suffolk Broads Act 1988.

1972 c. 70.

25. A joint committee constituted in accordance with section 102(1)(b) of the Local Government Act 1972.

26. A joint board which is continued in being by virtue of section 263(1) of the Local Government Act 1972.

27. A joint authority established under section 21 of the Local Government Act 1992.

1968 c. 73.

28. A Passenger Transport Executive for a passenger transport area within the meaning of Part II of the Transport Act 1968.

29. Transport for London.

30. The London Transport Users Committee.

31. A joint board the constituent members of which consist of any of the public authorities described in paragraphs 8, 9, 10, 12, 15, 16, 20 to 31, 57 and 58.

1995 c. 25.

32. A National Park authority established by an order under section 63 of the Environment Act 1995.

1990 c. 8.

33. A joint planning board constituted for an area in Wales outside a National Park by an order under section 2(1B) of the Town and Country Planning Act 1990.

34. A magistrates' court committee established under section 27 of the Justices 1997 c. 25.
of the Peace Act 1997.

35. The London Development Agency.

Northern Ireland

36. A district council within the meaning of the Local Government Act 1972 c. 9 (N.I.).
(Northern Ireland) 1972.

PART III

THE NATIONAL HEALTH SERVICE

England and Wales

37. A Health Authority established under section 8 of the National Health 1977 c. 49.
Service Act 1977.

38. A special health authority established under section 11 of the National
Health Service Act 1977.

39. A primary care trust established under section 16A of the National Health
Service Act 1977.

40. A National Health Service trust established under section 5 of the National 1990 c. 19.
Health Service and Community Care Act 1990.

41. A Community Health Council established under section 20 of the National
Health Service Act 1977.

42. The Dental Practice Board constituted under regulations made under
section 37 of the National Health Service Act 1977.

43. The Public Health Laboratory Service Board constituted under Schedule
3 to the National Health Service Act 1977.

44. Any person providing general medical services, general dental services,
general ophthalmic services or pharmaceutical services under Part II of the
National Health Service Act 1977, in respect of information relating to the
provision of those services.

45. Any person providing personal medical services or personal dental services
under arrangements made under section 28C of the National Health Service Act
1977, in respect of information relating to the provision of those services.

Northern Ireland

46. A Health and Social Services Board established under Article 16 of the
Health and Personal Social Services (Northern Ireland) Order 1972. S.I. 1972/1265
(N.I. 14).

47. A Health and Social Services Council established under Article 4 of the
Health and Personal Social Services (Northern Ireland) Order 1991. S.I. 1991/194 (N.I.
1).

48. A Health and Social Services Trust established under Article 10 of the
Health and Personal Social Services (Northern Ireland) Order 1991.

49. A special agency established under Article 3 of the Health and Personal S.I. 1990/247 (N.I.
Social Services (Special Agencies) (Northern Ireland) Order 1990. 3).

S.I. 1972/1265
(N.I. 14).

50. The Northern Ireland Central Services Agency for the Health and Social Services established under Article 26 of the Health and Personal Social Services (Northern Ireland) Order 1972.

51. Any person providing general medical services, general dental services, general ophthalmic services or pharmaceutical services under Part VI of the Health and Personal Social Services (Northern Ireland) Order 1972, in respect of information relating to the provision of those services.

PART IV

MAINTAINED SCHOOLS AND OTHER EDUCATIONAL INSTITUTIONS

England and Wales

1998 c. 56.

52. The governing body of a maintained school, within the meaning of the School Standards and Framework Act 1998.

53.—(1) The governing body of—

1992 c. 13.

(a) an institution within the further education sector,

(b) a university receiving financial support under section 65 of the Further and Higher Education Act 1992,

(c) an institution conducted by a higher education corporation,

(d) a designated institution for the purposes of Part II of the Further and Higher Education Act 1992 as defined by section 72(3) of that Act, or

(e) any college, school, hall or other institution of a university which falls within paragraph (b).

(2) In sub-paragraph (1)—

(a) "governing body" is to be interpreted in accordance with subsection (1) of section 90 of the Further and Higher Education Act 1992 but without regard to subsection (2) of that section,

(b) in paragraph (a), the reference to an institution within the further education sector is to be construed in accordance with section 91(3) of the Further and Higher Education Act 1992,

(c) in paragraph (c), "higher education corporation" has the meaning given by section 90(1) of that Act, and

(d) in paragraph (e) "college" includes any institution in the nature of a college.

Northern Ireland

54.—(1) The managers of—

S.I. 1986/594 (N.I. 3).

(a) a controlled school, voluntary school or grant-maintained integrated school within the meaning of Article 2(2) of the Education and Libraries (Northern Ireland) Order 1986, or

S.I. 1998/1759 (N.I. 13).

(b) a pupil referral unit as defined by Article 87(1) of the Education (Northern Ireland) Order 1998.

(2) In sub-paragraph (1) "managers" has the meaning given by Article 2(2) of the Education and Libraries (Northern Ireland) Order 1986.

55.—(1) The governing body of—

S.I. 1993/2810 (N.I. 12).

(a) a university receiving financial support under Article 30 of the Education and Libraries (Northern Ireland) Order 1993,

(b) a college of education maintained in pursuance of arrangements under Article 66(1) or in respect of which grants are paid under Article 66(2) or (3) of the Education and Libraries (Northern Ireland) Order 1986, or

(c) an institution of further education within the meaning of the Further Education (Northern Ireland) Order 1997.

S.I. 1997/1772 (N.I. 15).

(2) In sub-paragraph (1) "governing body" has the meaning given by Article 30(3) of the Education and Libraries (Northern Ireland) Order 1993.

S.I. 1993/2810 (N.I. 12).

56. Any person providing further education to whom grants, loans or other payments are made under Article 5(1)(b) of the Further Education (Northern Ireland) Order 1997.

PART V

POLICE

England and Wales

57. A police authority established under section 3 of the Police Act 1996.

1996 c. 16.

58. The Metropolitan Police Authority established under section 5B of the Police Act 1996.

59. A chief officer of police of a police force in England or Wales.

Northern Ireland

60. The Police Authority for Northern Ireland.

61. The Chief Constable of the Royal Ulster Constabulary.

Miscellaneous

62. The British Transport Police.

63. The Ministry of Defence Police established by section 1 of the Ministry of Defence Police Act 1987.

1987 c. 4.

64. Any person who—

(a) by virtue of any enactment has the function of nominating individuals who may be appointed as special constables by justices of the peace, and

(b) is not a public authority by virtue of any other provision of this Act,

in respect of information relating to the exercise by any person appointed on his nomination of the functions of a special constable.

PART VI

OTHER PUBLIC BODIES AND OFFICES: GENERAL

The Adjudicator for the Inland Revenue and Customs and Excise.

The Administration of Radioactive Substances Advisory Committee.

The Advisory Board on Family Law.

The Advisory Board on Restricted Patients.

The Advisory Board on the Registration of Homoeopathic Products.

The Advisory Committee for Cleaner Coal Technology.

The Advisory Committee for Disabled People in Employment and Training.

The Advisory Committee for the Public Lending Right.

The Advisory Committee for Wales (in relation to the Environment Agency).

The Advisory Committee on Advertising.

The Advisory Committee on Animal Feedingstuffs.

The Advisory Committee on Borderline Substances.

The Advisory Committee on Business and the Environment.

The Advisory Committee on Business Appointments.

The Advisory Committee on Conscientious Objectors.

The Advisory Committee on Consumer Products and the Environment.

The Advisory Committee on Dangerous Pathogens.

The Advisory Committee on Distinction Awards.

An Advisory Committee on General Commissioners of Income Tax.

The Advisory Committee on the Government Art Collection

The Advisory Committee on Hazardous Substances.

The Advisory Committee on Historic Wreck Sites.

An Advisory Committee on Justices of the Peace in England and Wales.

The Advisory Committee on the Microbiological Safety of Food.

The Advisory Committee on NHS Drugs.

The Advisory Committee on Novel Foods and Processes.

The Advisory Committee on Overseas Economic and Social Research.

The Advisory Committee on Packaging.

The Advisory Committee on Pesticides.

The Advisory Committee on Releases to the Environment.

The Advisory Council on Libraries.

The Advisory Council on the Misuse of Drugs.

The Advisory Council on Public Records.

The Advisory Group on Hepatitis.

The Advisory Panel on Standards for the Planning Inspectorate.

The Aerospace Committee.

An Agricultural Dwelling House Advisory Committee.

An Agricultural Wages Board for England and Wales.

An Agricultural Wages Committee.

The Agriculture and Environment Biotechnology Commission.

The Airborne Particles Expert Group.

The Alcohol Education and Research Council.

The Ancient Monuments Board for Wales.

The Animal Procedures Committee.

The Animal Welfare Advisory Committee.

The Apple and Pear Research Council.

The Armed Forces Pay Review Body.

The Arts Council of England.

The Arts Council of Wales.

The Audit Commission for Local Authorities and the National Health Service in England and Wales.

The Auditor General for Wales.

The Authorised Conveyancing Practitioners Board.

The Bank of England, in respect of information held for purposes other than those of its functions with respect to—

    (a) monetary policy,

    (b) financial operations intended to support financial institutions for the purposes of maintaining stability, and

    (c) the provision of private banking services and related services.

The Better Regulation Task Force.

The Biotechnology and Biological Sciences Research Council.

Any Board of Visitors established under section 6(2) of the Prison Act 1952.   1952 c. 52.

The Britain-Russia Centre and East-West Centre.

The British Association for Central and Eastern Europe.

The British Broadcasting Corporation, in respect of information held for purposes other than those of journalism, art or literature.

The British Coal Corporation.

The British Council.

The British Educational Communications and Technology Agency.

The British Hallmarking Council.

The British Library.

The British Museum.

The British Pharmacopoeia Commission.

The British Potato Council.

The British Railways Board.

British Shipbuilders.

The British Tourist Authority.

The British Waterways Board.

The British Wool Marketing Board.

The Broadcasting Standards Commission.

The Building Regulations Advisory Committee.

The Central Advisory Committee on War Pensions.

The Central Council for Education and Training in Social Work (UK).

The Central Rail Users' Consultative Committee.

The Channel Four Television Corporation, in respect of information held for purposes other than those of journalism, art or literature.

The Children and Family Court Advisory and Support Service.

The Civil Aviation Authority.

The Civil Justice Council.

The Civil Procedure Rule Committee.

The Civil Service Appeal Board.

The Civil Service Commissioners.

The Coal Authority.

The Commission for Architecture and the Built Environment.

The Commission for Health Improvement.

The Commission for Local Administration in England.

The Commission for Local Administration in Wales.

The Commission for Racial Equality.

The Commission for the New Towns.

The Commissioner for Integrated Transport.

The Commissioner for Public Appointments.

The Committee for Monitoring Agreements on Tobacco Advertising and Sponsorship.

The Committee of Investigation for Great Britain.

The Committee on Agricultural Valuation.

The Committee on Carcinogenicity of Chemicals in Food, Consumer Products and the Environment.

The Committee on Chemicals and Materials of Construction For Use in Public Water Supply and Swimming Pools.

The Committee on Medical Aspects of Food and Nutrition Policy.

The Committee on Medical Aspects of Radiation in the Environment.

The Committee on Mutagenicity of Chemicals in Food, Consumer Products and the Environment.

The Committee on Standards in Public Life.

The Committee on Toxicity of Chemicals in Food, Consumer Products and the Environment.

The Committee on the Medical Effects of Air Pollutants.

The Committee on the Safety of Medicines.

The Commonwealth Scholarship Commission in the United Kingdom.

The Community Development Foundation.

The Competition Commission, in relation to information held by it otherwise than as a tribunal.

The Construction Industry Training Board.

Consumer Communications for England.

The Consumer Panel.

The consumers' committee for Great Britain appointed under section 19 of the Agricultural Marketing Act 1958.

1958 c. 47.

The Council for Professions Supplementary to Medicine.

The Council for the Central Laboratory of the Research Councils.

The Council for Science and Technology.

The Council on Tribunals.

The Countryside Agency.

The Countryside Council for Wales.

The Covent Garden Market Authority.

The Criminal Cases Review Commission.

The Criminal Justice Consultative Council.

The Crown Court Rule Committee.

The Dartmoor Steering Group and Working Party.

The Darwin Advisory Committee.

The Defence Nuclear Safety Committee.

The Defence Scientific Advisory Council.

The Design Council.

The Development Awareness Working Group.

The Diplomatic Service Appeal Board.

The Disability Living Allowance Advisory Board.

The Disability Rights Commission.

The Disabled Persons Transport Advisory Committee.

The Economic and Social Research Council.

The Education Transfer Council.

The Energy Advisory Panel.

The Engineering Construction Industry Training Board.

The Engineering and Physical Sciences Research Council.

The English National Board for Nursing, Midwifery and Health Visiting.

English Nature.

The English Sports Council.

The English Tourist Board.

The Environment Agency.

The Equal Opportunities Commission.

The Expert Advisory Group on AIDS.

The Expert Group on Cryptosporidium in Water Supplies.

An Expert Panel on Air Quality Standards.

The Export Guarantees Advisory Council.

The Family Proceedings Rules Committee.

The Farm Animal Welfare Council.

The Fire Services Examination Board.

The Firearms Consultative Committee.

The Food Advisory Committee.

Food from Britain.

The Football Licensing Authority.

The Fuel Cell Advisory Panel.

The Further Education Funding Council for Wales.

The Gaming Board for Great Britain.

The Gas Consumers' Council.

The Gene Therapy Advisory Committee.

The General Chiropractic Council.

The General Dental Council.

The General Medical Council.

The General Osteopathic Council.

The Genetic Testing and Insurance Committee.

The Government Hospitality Advisory Committee for the Purchase of Wine.

The Government Chemist.

The Great Britain-China Centre.

The Health and Safety Commission.

The Health and Safety Executive.

The Health Service Commissioner for England.

The Health Service Commissioner for Wales.

Her Majesty's Chief Inspector of Schools in Wales.

The Higher Education Funding Council for England.

The Higher Education Funding Council for Wales.

The Hill Farming Advisory Committee.

The Hill Farming Advisory Sub-committee for Wales.

The Historic Buildings Council for Wales.

The Historic Buildings and Monuments Commission for England.

The Historic Royal Palaces Trust.

The Home-Grown Cereals Authority.

The Honorary Investment Advisory Committee.

The Horserace Betting Levy Board.

The Horserace Totalisator Board.

The Horticultural Development Council.

Horticulture Research International.

The House of Lords Appointments Commission.

1988 c. 50.   Any housing action trust established under Part III of the Housing Act 1988.

The Housing Corporation.

The Human Fertilisation and Embryology Authority.

The Human Genetics Commission.

The Immigration Services Commissioner.

The Imperial War Museum.

The Independent Board of Visitors for Military Corrective Training Centres.

The Independent Case Examiner for the Child Support Agency.

The Independent Living Funds.

The Independent Television Commission.

The Indian Family Pensions Funds Body of Commissioners.

The Industrial Development Advisory Board.

The Industrial Injuries Advisory Council.

The Information Commissioner.

The Inland Waterways Amenity Advisory Council.

The Insolvency Rules Committee.

The Insurance Brokers Registration Council.

Investors in People UK.

The Joint Committee on Vaccination and Immunisation.

The Joint Nature Conservation Committee.

The Joint Prison/Probation Accreditation Panel.

The Judicial Studies Board.

The Know-How Fund Advisory Board.

The Land Registration Rule Committee.

The Law Commission.

The Legal Services Commission.

The Legal Services Consultative Panel.

The Legal Services Ombudsman.

The Library and Information Services Council (Wales).

The Local Government Boundary Commission for Wales.

The Local Government Commission for England.

A local probation board established under section 4 of the Criminal Justice
      and Court Services Act 2000.   2000 c. 42.

The London Pensions Fund Authority.

The Low Pay Commission.

The Magistrates' Courts Rules Committee.

The Marshall Aid Commemoration Commission.

The Measurement Advisory Committee.

The Meat and Livestock Commission.

The Medical Practices Committee.

The Medical Research Council.

The Medical Workforce Standing Advisory Committee.

The Medicines Commission.

The Milk Development Council.

The Millennium Commission.

The Museum of London.

The National Army Museum.

The National Audit Office.

The National Biological Standards Board (UK).

The National Consumer Council.

The National Crime Squad.

The National Employers' Liaison Committee.

The National Endowment for Science, Technology and the Arts.

The National Expert Group on Transboundary Air Pollution.

The National Gallery.

The National Heritage Memorial Fund.

The National Library of Wales.

The National Lottery Charities Board.

The National Lottery Commission.

The National Maritime Museum.

The National Museum of Science and Industry.

The National Museums and Galleries of Wales.

The National Museums and Galleries on Merseyside.

The National Portrait Gallery.

The National Radiological Protection Board.

The Natural Environment Research Council.

The Natural History Museum.

The New Deal Task Force.

The New Opportunities Fund.

The Occupational Pensions Regulatory Authority.

The Oil and Pipelines Agency.

The OSO Board.

The Overseas Service Pensions Scheme Advisory Board.

The Panel on Standards for the Planning Inspectorate.

The Parliamentary Boundary Commission for England.

The Parliamentary Boundary Commission for Scotland.

The Parliamentary Boundary Commission for Wales.

The Parliamentary Commissioner for Administration.

The Parole Board.

The Particle Physics and Astronomy Research Council.

The Pensions Compensation Board.

The Pensions Ombudsman.

The Pharmacists' Review Panel.

The Place Names Advisory Committee.

The Poisons Board.

The Police Complaints Authority.

The Police Information Technology Organisation.

The Police Negotiating Board.

The Political Honours Scrutiny Committee.

The Post Office.

The Post Office Users' Councils for Scotland, Wales and Northern Ireland.

The Post Office Users' National Council.

The Property Advisory Group.

The Qualifications, Curriculum and Assessment Authority for Wales.

The Qualifications Curriculum Authority.

The Race Education and Employment Forum.

The Race Relations Forum.

The Radio Authority.

The Radioactive Waste Management Advisory Committee.

A Regional Cultural Consortium.

1998 c. 45.   Any regional development agency established under the Regional Development Agencies Act 1998, other than the London Development Agency.

Any regional flood defence committee.

The Registrar of Occupational and Personal Pension Schemes.

The Registrar of Public Lending Right.

Remploy Ltd.

The Renewable Energy Advisory Committee.

Resource: The Council for Museums, Archives and Libraries.

The Review Board for Government Contracts.

The Review Body for Nursing Staff, Midwives, Health Visitors and Professions Allied to Medicine.

The Review Body on Doctors and Dentists Remuneration.

The Reviewing Committee on the Export of Works of Art.

The Royal Air Force Museum.

The Royal Armouries.

The Royal Botanic Gardens, Kew.

The Royal Commission on Ancient and Historical Monuments of Wales.

The Royal Commission on Environmental Pollution.

The Royal Commission on Historical Manuscripts.

The Royal Military College of Science Advisory Council.

The Royal Mint Advisory Committee on the Design of Coins, Medals, Seals and Decorations.

The School Teachers' Review Body.

The Scientific Committee on Tobacco and Health.

The Scottish Advisory Committee on Telecommunications.

The Scottish Committee of the Council on Tribunals.

The Sea Fish Industry Authority.

The Senior Salaries Review Body.

The Sentencing Advisory Panel.

The Service Authority for the National Crime Squad.

Sianel Pedwar Cymru, in respect of information held for purposes other than those of journalism, art or literature.

Sir John Soane's Museum.

The Skills Task Force.

The social fund Commissioner appointed under section 65 of the Social 1992 c. 5. Security Administration Act 1992.

The Social Security Advisory Committee.

The Social Services Inspectorate for Wales Advisory Group.

The Spongiform Encephalopathy Advisory Committee.

The Sports Council for Wales.

The Standing Advisory Committee on Industrial Property.

The Standing Advisory Committee on Trunk Road Assessment.

The Standing Dental Advisory Committee.

The Standing Nursing and Midwifery Advisory Committee.

The Standing Medical Advisory Committee.

The Standing Pharmaceutical Advisory Committee.

The Steering Committee on Pharmacy Postgraduate Education.

The subsidence adviser appointed under section 46 of the Coal Industry 1994 c. 21. Act 1994.

The Substance Misuse Advisory Panel.

The Sustainable Development Commission.

The Sustainable Development Education Panel.

The Tate Gallery.

The Teacher Training Agency.

The Theatres Trust.

The Traffic Commissioners, in respect of information held by them otherwise than as a tribunal.

The Treasure Valuation Committee.

The UK Advisory Panel for Health Care Workers Infected with Bloodborne Viruses.

The UK Sports Council.

The United Kingdom Atomic Energy Authority.

The United Kingdom Central Council for Nursing, Midwifery and Health Visiting.

The United Kingdom Register of Organic Food Standards.

The United Kingdom Xenotransplantation Interim Regulatory Authority.

The Unlinked Anonymous Serosurveys Steering Group.

The Unrelated Live Transplant Regulatory Authority.

The Urban Regeneration Agency.

The Veterinary Products Committee.

The Victoria and Albert Museum.

The Wales New Deal Advisory Task Force.

The Wales Tourist Board.

The Wallace Collection.

The War Pensions Committees.

The Water Regulations Advisory Committee.

The Welsh Administration Ombudsman.

The Welsh Advisory Committee on Telecommunications.

The Welsh Committee for Professional Development of Pharmacy.

The Welsh Dental Committee.

The Welsh Development Agency.

The Welsh Industrial Development Advisory Board.

The Welsh Language Board.

The Welsh Medical Committee.

The Welsh National Board for Nursing, Midwifery and Health Visiting.

The Welsh Nursing and Midwifery Committee.

The Welsh Optometric Committee.

The Welsh Pharmaceutical Committee.

The Welsh Scientific Advisory Committee.

The Westminster Foundation for Democracy.

The Wilton Park Academic Council.

The Wine Standards Board of the Vintners' Company.

The Women's National Commission.

The Youth Justice Board for England and Wales.

The Zoos Forum.

Part VII

Other public bodies and offices: Northern Ireland

An Advisory Committee on General Commissioners of Income Tax (Northern Ireland).

The Advisory Committee on Justices of the Peace in Northern Ireland.

The Advisory Committee on Juvenile Court Lay Panel (Northern Ireland).

The Advisory Committee on Pesticides for Northern Ireland.

The Agricultural Research Institute of Northern Ireland.

The Agricultural Wages Board for Northern Ireland.

The Arts Council of Northern Ireland.

The Assembly Ombudsman for Northern Ireland.

The Board of Trustees of National Museums and Galleries of Northern Ireland.

Boards of Visitors and Visiting Committees.

The Boundary Commission for Northern Ireland.

The Charities Advisory Committee.

The Chief Electoral Officer for Northern Ireland.

The Civil Service Commissioners for Northern Ireland.

The Commissioner for Public Appointments for Northern Ireland.

The Construction Industry Training Board.

The consultative Civic Forum referred to in section 56(4) of the Northern Ireland Act 1998.   1998 c. 47.

The Council for Catholic Maintained Schools.

The Council for Nature Conservation and the Countryside.

The County Court Rules Committee (Northern Ireland).

The Disability Living Allowance Advisory Board for Northern Ireland.

The Distinction and Meritorious Service Awards Committee.

The Drainage Council for Northern Ireland.

An Education and Library Board established under Article 3 of the Education and Libraries (Northern Ireland) Order 1986.   S.I. 1986/594 (N.I. 3).

Enterprise Ulster.

The Equality Commission for Northern Ireland.

The Family Proceedings Rules Committee (Northern Ireland).

The Fire Authority for Northern Ireland.

The Fisheries Conservancy Board for Northern Ireland.

The General Consumer Council for Northern Ireland.

The Health and Safety Agency for Northern Ireland.

The Historic Buildings Council.

The Historic Monuments Council.

The Independent Assessor of Military Complaints Procedures in Northern Ireland.

The Independent Reviewer of the Northern Ireland (Emergency Provisions) Act.

The Independent Commissioner for Holding Centres.

The Industrial Development Board for Northern Ireland.

The Industrial Research and Technology Unit.

The Juvenile Justice Board.

The Labour Relations Agency.

The Laganside Corporation.

The Law Reform Advisory Committee for Northern Ireland.

The Lay Observer for Northern Ireland.

The Legal Aid Advisory Committee (Northern Ireland).

The Livestock & Meat Commission for Northern Ireland.

The Local Enterprise Development Unit.

The Local Government Staff Commission.

The Magistrates' Courts Rules Committee (Northern Ireland).

The Mental Health Commission for Northern Ireland.

The Northern Ireland Advisory Committee on Telecommunications.

The Northern Ireland Audit Office.

The Northern Ireland Building Regulations Advisory Committee.

The Northern Ireland Civil Service Appeal Board.

The Northern Ireland Commissioner for Complaints.

The Northern Ireland Community Relations Council.

The Northern Ireland Consumer Committee for Electricity.

The Northern Ireland Council for the Curriculum, Examinations and Assessment.

The Northern Ireland Council for Postgraduate Medical and Dental Education.

The Northern Ireland Crown Court Rules Committee.

The Northern Ireland Economic Council.

The Northern Ireland Fishery Harbour Authority.

The Northern Ireland Higher Education Council.

The Northern Ireland Housing Executive.

The Northern Ireland Human Rights Commission.

The Northern Ireland Insolvency Rules Committee.

The Northern Ireland Local Government Officers' Superannuation Committee.

The Northern Ireland Museums Council.

The Northern Ireland Pig Production Development Committee.

The Northern Ireland Supreme Court Rules Committee.

The Northern Ireland Tourist Board.

The Northern Ireland Transport Holding Company.

The Northern Ireland Water Council.

The Parades Commission.

The Police Ombudsman for Northern Ireland.

The Probation Board for Northern Ireland.

The Rural Development Council for Northern Ireland.

1998 c. 35.

The Sentence Review Commissioners appointed under section 1 of the Northern Ireland (Sentences) Act 1998.

S.I. 1998/1506 (N.I.10).

The social fund Commissioner appointed under Article 37 of the Social Security (Northern Ireland) Order 1998.

The Sports Council for Northern Ireland.

The Staff Commission for Education and Library Boards.

The Statistics Advisory Committee.

The Statute Law Committee for Northern Ireland.

The Training and Employment Agency.

Ulster Supported Employment Ltd.

The Youth Council for Northern Ireland.

Section 18(4).

SCHEDULE 2

The Commissioner and the Tribunal

Part I

Provision consequential on s. 18(1) and (2)

General

1.—(1) Any reference in any enactment, instrument or document to the Data Protection Commissioner or the Data Protection Registrar shall be construed, in relation to any time after the commencement of section 18(1), as a reference to the Information Commissioner.

(2) Any reference in any enactment, instrument or document to the Data Protection Tribunal shall be construed, in relation to any time after the commencement of section 18(2), as a reference to the Information Tribunal.

2.—(1) Any reference in this Act or in any instrument under this Act to the Commissioner shall be construed, in relation to any time before the commencement of section 18(1), as a reference to the Data Protection Commissioner.

(2) Any reference in this Act or in any instrument under this Act to the Tribunal shall be construed, in relation to any time before the commencement of section 18(2), as a reference to the Data Protection Tribunal.

Public Records Act 1958 (c. 51)

3.—(1) In Part II of the Table in paragraph 3 of Schedule 1 to the Public Records Act 1958 (definition of public records), the entry relating to the Data Protection Commissioner is omitted and there is inserted at the appropriate place—

"Information Commissioner."

(2) In paragraph 4(1) of that Schedule, for paragraph (nn) there is substituted—

"(nn) records of the Information Tribunal;".

Parliamentary Commissioner Act 1967 (c. 13)

4. In Schedule 2 to the Parliamentary Commissioner Act 1967 (departments etc. subject to investigation), the entry relating to the Data Protection Commissioner is omitted and there is inserted at the appropriate place—

"Information Commissioner".

5. In Schedule 4 to that Act (tribunals exercising administrative functions), for the entry relating to the Data Protection Tribunal there is substituted—

"Information Tribunal constituted under section 6 of the Data Protection Act 1998."

Superannuation Act 1972 (c. 11)

6. In Schedule 1 to the Superannuation Act 1972 (employment with superannuation scheme), for "Data Protection Commissioner" there is substituted "Information Commissioner".

Consumer Credit Act 1974 (c. 39)

7. In section 159 of the Consumer Credit Act 1974 (correction of wrong information), in subsections (7) and (8)(b), for "Data Protection Commissioner", in both places where it occurs, there is substituted "Information Commissioner".

House of Commons Disqualification Act 1975 (c. 24)

8.—(1) In Part II of Schedule 1 to the House of Commons Disqualification Act 1975 (bodies whose members are disqualified), the entry relating to the Data Protection Tribunal is omitted and there is inserted at the appropriate place—

"The Information Tribunal".

(2) In Part III of that Schedule (disqualifying offices), the entry relating to the Data Protection Commissioner is omitted and there is inserted at the appropriate place—

"The Information Commissioner".

Northern Ireland Assembly Disqualification Act 1975 (c. 25)

9.—(1) In Part II of Schedule 1 to the Northern Ireland Assembly Disqualification Act 1975 (bodies whose members are disqualified), the entry relating to the Data Protection Tribunal is omitted and there is inserted at the appropriate place—

"The Information Tribunal".

(2) In Part III of that Schedule (disqualifying offices), the entry relating to the Data Protection Commissioner is omitted and there is inserted at the appropriate place—

"The Information Commissioner".

Tribunals and Inquiries Act 1992 (c. 53)

10. In paragraph 14 of Part I of Schedule 1 to the Tribunals and Inquiries Act 1992 (tribunals under direct supervision of Council on Tribunals)—

(a) in sub-paragraph (a), for "The Data Protection Commissioner" there is substituted "The Information Commissioner", and

(b) for sub-paragraph (b) there is substituted—

"(b) the Information Tribunal constituted under that section, in respect of its jurisdiction under—

(i) section 48 of that Act, and

(ii) section 57 of the Freedom of Information Act 2000."

Judicial Pensions and Retirement Act 1993 (c. 8)

11. In Schedule 5 to the Judicial Pensions and Retirement Act 1993 (retirement provisions: the relevant offices), in the entry relating to the chairman and deputy chairman of the Data Protection Tribunal, for "the Data Protection Tribunal" there is substituted "the Information Tribunal".

12. In Schedule 7 to that Act (retirement dates: transitional provisions), in paragraph 5(5)(xxvi) for "the Data Protection Tribunal" there is substituted "the Information Tribunal".

Data Protection Act 1998 (c. 29)

13.—(1) Section 6 of the Data Protection Act 1998 (the Data Protection Commissioner and the Data Protection Tribunal) is amended as follows.

(2) For subsection (1) there is substituted—

"(1) For the purposes of this Act and of the Freedom of Information Act 2000 there shall be an officer known as the Information Commissioner (in this Act referred to as "the Commissioner")."

(3) For subsection (3) there is substituted—

"(3) For the purposes of this Act and of the Freedom of Information Act 2000 there shall be a tribunal known as the Information Tribunal (in this Act referred to as "the Tribunal")."

14. In section 70(1) of that Act (supplementary definitions)—

(a) in the definition of "the Commissioner", for "the Data Protection Commissioner" there is substituted "the Information Commissioner", and

(b) in the definition of "the Tribunal", for "the Data Protection Tribunal" there is substituted "the Information Tribunal".

15.—(1) Schedule 5 to that Act (the Data Protection Commissioner and the Data Protection Tribunal) is amended as follows.

(2) In paragraph 1(1), for "Data Protection Commissioner" there is substituted "Information Commissioner".

(3) Part III shall cease to have effect.

PART II

A<small>MENDMENTS RELATING TO EXTENSION OF FUNCTIONS OF</small> C<small>OMMISSIONER AND</small> T<small>RIBUNAL</small>

Interests represented by lay members of Tribunal

16. In section 6(6) of the Data Protection Act 1998 (lay members of Tribunal)— 1998 c. 29.

(a) for the word "and" at the end of paragraph (a) there is substituted—

"(aa) persons to represent the interests of those who make requests for information under the Freedom of Information Act 2000,", and

(b) after paragraph (b) there is inserted "and

(bb) persons to represent the interests of public authorities."

Expenses incurred under this Act excluded in calculating fees

17. In section 26(2) of that Act (fees regulations), in paragraph (a)—

(a) after "functions" there is inserted "under this Act", and

(b) after "Tribunal" there is inserted "so far as attributable to their functions under this Act".

Information provided to Commissioner or Tribunal

18. In section 58 of that Act (disclosure of information to Commissioner or Tribunal), after "this Act" there is inserted "or the Freedom of Information Act 2000".

19.—(1) Section 59 of that Act (confidentiality of information) is amended as follows.

(2) In subsections (1) and (2), for "this Act", wherever occurring, there is substituted "the information Acts".

(3) After subsection (3) there is inserted—

"(4) In this section "the information Acts" means this Act and the Freedom of Information Act 2000."

Deputy commissioners

20.—(1) Paragraph 4 of Schedule 5 to that Act (officers and staff) is amended as follows.

(2) In sub-paragraph (1)(a), after "a deputy commissioner" there is inserted "or two deputy commissioners".

(3) After sub-paragraph (1) there is inserted—

"(1A) The Commissioner shall, when appointing any second deputy commissioner, specify which of the Commissioner's functions are to be performed, in the circumstances referred to in paragraph 5(1), by each of the deputy commissioners."

Exercise of Commissioner's functions by others

21.—(1) Paragraph 5 of Schedule 5 to that Act (exercise of functions of Commissioner during vacancy etc.) is amended as follows.

(2) In sub-paragraph (1)—

    (a) after "deputy commissioner" there is inserted "or deputy commissioners", and

    (b) after "this Act" there is inserted "or the Freedom of Information Act 2000".

(3) In sub-paragraph (2) after "this Act" there is inserted "or the Freedom of Information Act 2000".

Money

22. In paragraph 9(1) of Schedule 5 to that Act (money) for "or section 159 of the Consumer Credit Act 1974" there is substituted ", under section 159 of the Consumer Credit Act 1974 or under the Freedom of Information Act 2000".

Section 55.

SCHEDULE 3

POWERS OF ENTRY AND INSPECTION

Issue of warrants

1.—(1) If a circuit judge is satisfied by information on oath supplied by the Commissioner that there are reasonable grounds for suspecting—

    (a) that a public authority has failed or is failing to comply with—

        (i) any of the requirements of Part I of this Act,

        (ii) so much of a decision notice as requires steps to be taken, or

        (iii) an information notice or an enforcement notice, or

    (b) that an offence under section 77 has been or is being committed,

and that evidence of such a failure to comply or of the commission of the offence is to be found on any premises specified in the information, he may, subject to paragraph 2, grant a warrant to the Commissioner.

(2) A warrant issued under sub-paragraph (1) shall authorise the Commissioner or any of his officers or staff at any time within seven days of the date of the warrant—

    (a) to enter and search the premises,

    (b) to inspect and seize any documents or other material found there which may be such evidence as is mentioned in that sub-paragraph, and

    (c) to inspect, examine, operate and test any equipment found there in which information held by the public authority may be recorded.

2.—(1) A judge shall not issue a warrant under this Schedule unless he is satisfied—

    (a) that the Commissioner has given seven days' notice in writing to the occupier of the premises in question demanding access to the premises, and

    (b) that either—

        (i) access was demanded at a reasonable hour and was unreasonably refused, or

(ii) although entry to the premises was granted, the occupier unreasonably refused to comply with a request by the Commissioner or any of the Commissioner's officers or staff to permit the Commissioner or the officer or member of staff to do any of the things referred to in paragraph 1(2), and

(c) that the occupier, has, after the refusal, been notified by the Commissioner of the application for the warrant and has had an opportunity of being heard by the judge on the question whether or not it should be issued.

(2) Sub-paragraph (1) shall not apply if the judge is satisfied that the case is one of urgency or that compliance with those provisions would defeat the object of the entry.

3. A judge who issues a warrant under this Schedule shall also issue two copies of it and certify them clearly as copies.

Execution of warrants

4. A person executing a warrant issued under this Schedule may use such reasonable force as may be necessary.

5. A warrant issued under this Schedule shall be executed at a reasonable hour unless it appears to the person executing it that there are grounds for suspecting that the evidence in question would not be found if it were so executed.

6.—(1) If the premises in respect of which a warrant is issued under this Schedule are occupied by a public authority and any officer or employee of the authority is present when the warrant is executed, he shall be shown the warrant and supplied with a copy of it; and if no such officer or employee is present a copy of the warrant shall be left in a prominent place on the premises.

(2) If the premises in respect of which a warrant is issued under this Schedule are occupied by a person other than a public authority and he is present when the warrant is executed, he shall be shown the warrant and supplied with a copy of it; and if that person is not present a copy of the warrant shall be left in a prominent place on the premises.

7.—(1) A person seizing anything in pursuance of a warrant under this Schedule shall give a receipt for it if asked to do so.

(2) Anything so seized may be retained for so long as is necessary in all the circumstances but the person in occupation of the premises in question shall be given a copy of anything that is seized if he so requests and the person executing the warrant considers that it can be done without undue delay.

Matters exempt from inspection and seizure

8. The powers of inspection and seizure conferred by a warrant issued under this Schedule shall not be exercisable in respect of information which is exempt information by virtue of section 23(1) or 24(1).

9.—(1) Subject to the provisions of this paragraph, the powers of inspection and seizure conferred by a warrant issued under this Schedule shall not be exercisable in respect of—

(a) any communication between a professional legal adviser and his client in connection with the giving of legal advice to the client with respect to his obligations, liabilities or rights under this Act, or

(b) any communication between a professional legal adviser and his client, or between such an adviser or his client and any other person, made in connection with or in contemplation of proceedings under or arising out of this Act (including proceedings before the Tribunal) and for the purposes of such proceedings.

(2) Sub-paragraph (1) applies also to—

(a) any copy or other record of any such communication as is there mentioned, and

(b) any document or article enclosed with or referred to in any such communication if made in connection with the giving of any advice or, as the case may be, in connection with or in contemplation of and for the purposes of such proceedings as are there mentioned.

(3) This paragraph does not apply to anything in the possession of any person other than the professional legal adviser or his client or to anything held with the intention of furthering a criminal purpose.

(4) In this paragraph references to the client of a professional legal adviser include references to any person representing such a client.

10. If the person in occupation of any premises in respect of which a warrant is issued under this Schedule objects to the inspection or seizure under the warrant of any material on the grounds that it consists partly of matters in respect of which those powers are not exercisable, he shall, if the person executing the warrant so requests, furnish that person with a copy of so much of the material in relation to which the powers are exercisable.

Return of warrants

11. A warrant issued under this Schedule shall be returned to the court from which it was issued—

(a) after being executed, or

(b) if not executed within the time authorised for its execution;

and the person by whom any such warrant is executed shall make an endorsement on it stating what powers have been exercised by him under the warrant.

Offences

12. Any person who—

(a) intentionally obstructs a person in the execution of a warrant issued under this Schedule, or

(b) fails without reasonable excuse to give any person executing such a warrant such assistance as he may reasonably require for the execution of the warrant,

is guilty of an offence.

Vessels, vehicles etc.

13. In this Schedule "premises" includes any vessel, vehicle, aircraft or hovercraft, and references to the occupier of any premises include references to the person in charge of any vessel, vehicle, aircraft or hovercraft.

Scotland and Northern Ireland

14. In the application of this Schedule to Scotland—

   (a) for any reference to a circuit judge there is substituted a reference to the sheriff, and

   (b) for any reference to information on oath there is substituted a reference to evidence on oath.

15. In the application of this Schedule to Northern Ireland—

   (a) for any reference to a circuit judge there is substituted a reference to a county court judge, and

   (b) for any reference to information on oath there is substituted a reference to a complaint on oath.

SCHEDULE 4

APPEAL PROCEEDINGS: AMENDMENTS OF SCHEDULE 6 TO DATA PROTECTION ACT 1998

Section 61(1).

Constitution of Tribunal in national security cases

1. In paragraph 2(1) of Schedule 6 to the Data Protection Act 1998 (constitution of Tribunal in national security cases), at the end there is inserted "or under section 60(1) or (4) of the Freedom of Information Act 2000".

1998 c. 29.

2. For paragraph 3 of that Schedule there is substituted—

   "3. The Tribunal shall be duly constituted—

   (a) for an appeal under section 28(4) or (6) in any case where the application of paragraph 6(1) is excluded by rules under paragraph 7, or

   (b) for an appeal under section 60(1) or (4) of the Freedom of Information Act 2000,

   if it consists of three of the persons designated under paragraph 2(1), of whom one shall be designated by the Lord Chancellor to preside."

Constitution of Tribunal in other cases

3.—(1) Paragraph 4 of that Schedule (constitution of Tribunal in other cases) is amended as follows.

(2) After sub-paragraph (1) there is inserted—

   "(1A) Subject to any rules made under paragraph 7, the Tribunal shall be duly constituted for an appeal under section 57(1) or (2) of the Freedom of Information Act 2000 if it consists of—

   (a) the chairman or a deputy chairman (who shall preside), and

   (b) an equal number of the members appointed respectively in accordance with paragraphs (aa) and (bb) of section 6(6)."

(3) In sub-paragraph (2), after "(1)" there is inserted "or (1A)".

Rules of procedure

4.—(1) Paragraph 7 of that Schedule (rules of procedure) is amended as follows.

(2) In sub-paragraph (1), for the words from "regulating" onwards there is substituted "regulating—

(a) the exercise of the rights of appeal conferred—

(i) by sections 28(4) and (6) and 48, and

(ii) by sections 57(1) and (2) and section 60(1) and (4) of the Freedom of Information Act 2000, and

(b) the practice and procedure of the Tribunal."

(3) In sub-paragraph (2), after paragraph (a) there is inserted—

"(aa) for the joinder of any other person as a party to any proceedings on an appeal under the Freedom of Information Act 2000,

(ab) for the hearing of an appeal under this Act with an appeal under the Freedom of Information Act 2000,".

Section 67.

SCHEDULE 5

AMENDMENTS OF PUBLIC RECORDS LEGISLATION

PART I

AMENDMENTS OF PUBLIC RECORDS ACT 1958

Functions of Advisory Council on Public Records

1958 c. 51.

1. In section 1 of the Public Records Act 1958 (general responsibility of the Lord Chancellor for public records), after subsection (2) there is inserted—

"(2A) The matters on which the Advisory Council on Public Records may advise the Lord Chancellor include matters relating to the application of the Freedom of Information Act 2000 to information contained in public records which are historical records within the meaning of Part VI of that Act."

Access to public records

2.—(1) Section 5 of that Act (access to public records) is amended in accordance with this paragraph.

(2) Subsections (1) and (2) are omitted.

(3) For subsection (3) there is substituted—

"(3) It shall be the duty of the Keeper of Public Records to arrange that reasonable facilities are available to the public for inspecting and obtaining copies of those public records in the Public Record Office which fall to be disclosed in accordance with the Freedom of Information Act 2000."

(4) Subsection (4) and, in subsection (5), the words from "and subject to" to the end are omitted.

3. Schedule 2 of that Act (enactments prohibiting disclosure of information obtained from the public) is omitted.

Power to extend meaning of "public records"

4. In Schedule 1 to that Act (definition of public records) after the Table at the end of paragraph 3 there is inserted—

"3A.—(1) Her Majesty may by Order in Council amend the Table at the end of paragraph 3 of this Schedule by adding to either Part of the Table an entry relating to any body or establishment—

(a) which, at the time when the Order is made, is specified in Schedule 2 to the Parliamentary Commissioner Act 1967 (departments, etc. subject to investigation), or

SCH. 5

(b) in respect of which an entry could, at that time, be added to Schedule 2 to that Act by an Order in Council under section 4 of that Act (which confers power to amend that Schedule).

(2) An Order in Council under this paragraph may relate to a specified body or establishment or to bodies or establishments falling within a specified description.

(3) An Order in Council under this paragraph shall be subject to annulment in pursuance of a resolution of either House of Parliament."

PART II

AMENDMENT OF PUBLIC RECORDS ACT (NORTHERN IRELAND) 1923

5. After section 5 of the Public Records Act (Northern Ireland) 1923 (deposit of documents in Record Office by trustees or other persons) there is inserted— 1923 c. 20 (N.I.).

"Access to public records

5A. It shall be the duty of the Deputy Keeper of the Records of Northern Ireland to arrange that reasonable facilities are available to the public for inspecting and obtaining copies of those public records in the Public Record Office of Northern Ireland which fall to be disclosed in accordance with the Freedom of Information Act 2000."

SCHEDULE 6

Section 73.

FURTHER AMENDMENTS OF DATA PROTECTION ACT 1998

Request by data controller for further information

1. In section 7 of the Data Protection Act 1998 (right of access to personal data), for subsection (3) there is substituted— 1998 c. 29.

"(3) Where a data controller—

(a) reasonably requires further information in order to satisfy himself as to the identity of the person making a request under this section and to locate the information which that person seeks, and

(b) has informed him of that requirement,

the data controller is not obliged to comply with the request unless he is supplied with that further information.

Parliament

2. After section 35 of that Act there is inserted—

"Parliamentary privilege.

35A. Personal data are exempt from—

(a) the first data protection principle, except to the extent to which it requires compliance with the conditions in Schedules 2 and 3,

(b) the second, third, fourth and fifth data protection principles,

(c) section 7, and

(d) sections 10 and 14(1) to (3),

if the exemption is required for the purpose of avoiding an infringement of the privileges of either House of Parliament."

3. After section 63 of that Act there is inserted—

"Application to Parliament.   63A.—(1) Subject to the following provisions of this section and to section 35A, this Act applies to the processing of personal data by or on behalf of either House of Parliament as it applies to the processing of personal data by other persons.

(2) Where the purposes for which and the manner in which any personal data are, or are to be, processed are determined by or on behalf of the House of Commons, the data controller in respect of those data for the purposes of this Act shall be the Corporate Officer of that House.

(3) Where the purposes for which and the manner in which any personal data are, or are to be, processed are determined by or on behalf of the House of Lords, the data controller in respect of those data for the purposes of this Act shall be the Corporate Officer of that House.

(4) Nothing in subsection (2) or (3) is to be taken to render the Corporate Officer of the House of Commons or the Corporate Officer of the House of Lords liable to prosecution under this Act, but section 55 and paragraph 12 of Schedule 9 shall apply to a person acting on behalf of either House as they apply to any other person."

4. In Schedule 2 to that Act (conditions relevant for the purposes of the first data protection principle: processing of any personal data) in paragraph 5 after paragraph (a) there is inserted—

"(aa) for the exercise of any functions of either House of Parliament,".

5. In Schedule 3 to that Act (conditions relevant for the purposes of the first data protection principle: processing of sensitive personal data) in paragraph 7 after paragraph (a) there is inserted—

"(aa) for the exercise of any functions of either House of Parliament,".

Honours

6. In Schedule 7 to that Act (miscellaneous exemptions) in paragraph 3(b) (honours) after "honour" there is inserted "or dignity".

Legal professional privilege

7. In paragraph 10 of that Schedule (legal professional privilege), for the words "or, in Scotland, to confidentiality as between client and professional legal adviser," there is substituted "or, in Scotland, to confidentiality of communications".

Extension of transitional exemption

8. In Schedule 14 to that Act (transitional provisions), in paragraph 2(1) (which confers transitional exemption from the prohibition on processing without registration on those registered under the Data Protection Act 1984) the words "or, if earlier, 24th October 2001" are omitted.

SCHEDULE 7

DISCLOSURE OF INFORMATION BY OMBUDSMEN

The Parliamentary Commissioner for Administration

1. At the end of section 11 of the Parliamentary Commissioner Act 1967 (provision for secrecy of information) there is inserted—

"(5) Information obtained from the Information Commissioner by virtue of section 76(1) of the Freedom of Information Act 2000 shall be treated for the purposes of subsection (2) of this section as obtained for the purposes of an investigation under this Act and, in relation to such information, the reference in paragraph (a) of that subsection to the investigation shall have effect as a reference to any investigation."

2. After section 11A of that Act there is inserted—

"Disclosure of information by Parliamentary Commissioner to Information Commissioner.

11AA.—(1) The Commissioner may disclose to the Information Commissioner any information obtained by, or furnished to, the Commissioner under or for the purposes of this Act if the information appears to the Commissioner to relate to—

    (a) a matter in respect of which the Information Commissioner could exercise any power conferred by—

        (i) Part V of the Data Protection Act 1998 (enforcement),

        (ii) section 48 of the Freedom of Information Act 2000 (practice recommendations), or

        (iii) Part IV of that Act (enforcement), or

    (b) the commission of an offence under—

        (i) any provision of the Data Protection Act 1998 other than paragraph 12 of Schedule 9 (obstruction of execution of warrant), or

        (ii) section 77 of the Freedom of Information Act 2000 (offence of altering etc. records with intent to prevent disclosure).

(2) Nothing in section 11(2) of this Act shall apply in relation to the disclosure of information in accordance with this section."

The Commissions for Local Administration in England and Wales

3. In section 32 of the Local Government Act 1974 (law of defamation, and disclosure of information) after subsection (6) there is inserted—

"(7) Information obtained from the Information Commissioner by virtue of section 76 of the Freedom of Information Act 2000 shall be treated for the purposes of subsection (2) above as obtained for the purposes of an investigation under this Part of this Act and, in relation to such information, the reference in paragraph (a) of that subsection to the investigation shall have effect as a reference to any investigation."

4. After section 33 of that Act there is inserted—

"Disclosure of information by Local Commissioner to Information Commissioner.

33A.—(1) A Local Commissioner may disclose to the Information Commissioner any information obtained by, or furnished to, the Local Commissioner under or for the purposes of this Part of this Act if the information appears to the Local Commissioner to relate to—

(a) a matter in respect of which the Information Commissioner could exercise any power conferred by—

(i) Part V of the Data Protection Act 1998 (enforcement),

(ii) section 48 of the Freedom of Information Act 2000 (practice recommendations), or

(iii) Part IV of that Act (enforcement), or

(b) the commission of an offence under—

(i) any provision of the Data Protection Act 1998 other than paragraph 12 of Schedule 9 (obstruction of execution of warrant), or

(ii) section 77 of the Freedom of Information Act 2000 (offence of altering etc. records with intent to prevent disclosure).

(2) Nothing in section 32(2) of this Act shall apply in relation to the disclosure of information in accordance with this section."

The Health Service Commissioners

1993 c. 46.

5. At the end of section 15 of the Health Service Commissioners Act 1993 (confidentiality of information) there is inserted—

"(4) Information obtained from the Information Commissioner by virtue of section 76 of the Freedom of Information Act 2000 shall be treated for the purposes of subsection (1) as obtained for the purposes of an investigation and, in relation to such information, the reference in paragraph (a) of that subsection to the investigation shall have effect as a reference to any investigation."

6. After section 18 of that Act there is inserted—

"Disclosure of information to Information Commissioner.

18A.—(1) The Health Service Commissioner for England or the Health Service Commissioner for Wales may disclose to the Information Commissioner any information obtained by, or furnished to, the Health Service Commissioner under or for the purposes of this Act if the information appears to the Health Service Commissioner to relate to—

(a) a matter in respect of which the Information Commissioner could exercise any power conferred by—

(i) Part V of the Data Protection Act 1998 (enforcement),

(ii) section 48 of the Freedom of Information Act 2000 (practice recommendations), or

(iii) Part IV of that Act (enforcement), or

(b) the commission of an offence under—

(i) any provision of the Data Protection Act 1998 other than paragraph 12 of Schedule 9 (obstruction of execution of warrant), or

(ii) section 77 of the Freedom of Information Act 2000 (offence of altering etc. records with intent to prevent disclosure).

(3) Nothing in section 15 (confidentiality of information) applies in relation to the disclosure of information in accordance with this section."

The Welsh Administration Ombudsman

7. In Schedule 9 to the Government of Wales Act 1998 (the Welsh Administration Ombudsman), at the end of paragraph 25 (confidentiality of information) there is inserted—

1998 c. 38.

"(5) Information obtained from the Information Commissioner by virtue of section 76 of the Freedom of Information Act 2000 shall be treated for the purposes of sub-paragraph (1) as obtained for the purposes of an investigation and, in relation to such information, the reference in paragraph (a) of that subsection to the investigation shall have effect as a reference to any investigation."

8. After paragraph 27 of that Schedule there is inserted—

"Disclosure of information to Information Commissioner

28.—(1) The Welsh Administration Ombudsman may disclose to the Information Commissioner any information obtained by, or furnished to, the Welsh Administration Ombudsman under or for the purposes of this Schedule if the information appears to the Welsh Administration Ombudsman to relate to—

(a) a matter in respect of which the Information Commissioner could exercise any power conferred by—

(i) Part V of the Data Protection Act 1998 (enforcement),

(ii) section 48 of the Freedom of Information Act 2000 (practice recommendations), or

(iii) Part IV of that Act (enforcement), or

(b) the commission of an offence under—

(i) any provision of the Data Protection Act 1998 other than paragraph 12 of Schedule 9 (obstruction of execution of warrant), or

(ii) section 77 of the Freedom of Information Act 2000 (offence of altering etc. records with intent to prevent disclosure).

(2) Nothing in paragraph 25(1) applies in relation to the disclosure of information in accordance with this paragraph."

The Northern Ireland Commissioner for Complaints

9. At the end of Article 21 of the Commissioner for Complaints (Northern Ireland) Order 1996 (disclosure of information by Commissioner) there is inserted—

S.I. 1996/1297 (N.I. 7).

"(5) Information obtained from the Information Commissioner by virtue of section 76 of the Freedom of Information Act 2000 shall be treated for the purposes of paragraph (1) as obtained for the purposes of an investigation under this Order and, in relation to such information, the reference in paragraph (1)(a) to the investigation shall have effect as a reference to any investigation."

10. After that Article there is inserted—

"Disclosure of information to Information Commissioner

21A.—(1) The Commissioner may disclose to the Information Commissioner any information obtained by, or furnished to, the Commissioner under or for the purposes of this Order if the information appears to the Commissioner to relate to—

(a) a matter in respect of which the Information Commissioner could exercise any power conferred by—

(i) Part V of the Data Protection Act 1998 (enforcement),

(ii) section 48 of the Freedom of Information Act 2000 (practice recommendations), or

(iii) Part IV of that Act (enforcement), or

(b) the commission of an offence under—

(i) any provision of the Data Protection Act 1998 other than paragraph 12 of Schedule 9 (obstruction of execution of warrant), or

(ii) section 77 of the Freedom of Information Act 2000 (offence of altering etc. records with intent to prevent disclosure).

(2) Nothing in Article 21(1) applies in relation to the disclosure of information in accordance with this Article."

The Assembly Ombudsman for Northern Ireland

S.I. 1996/1298   11. At the end of Article 19 of the Ombudsman (Northern Ireland) Order 1996
(N.I. 8).   there is inserted—

"(5) Information obtained from the Information Commissioner by virtue of section 76 of the Freedom of Information Act 2000 shall be treated for the purposes of paragraph (1) as obtained for the purposes of an investigation under this Order and, in relation to such information, the reference in paragraph (1)(a) to the investigation shall have effect as a reference to any investigation."

12. After that Article there is inserted—

"Disclosure of information to Information Commissioner

19A.—(1) The Ombudsman may disclose to the Information Commissioner any information obtained by, or furnished to, the Omubudsman under or for the purposes of this Order if the information appears to the Ombudsman to relate to—

(a) a matter in respect of which the Information Commissioner could exercise any power conferred by—

(i) Part V of the Data Protection Act 1998 (enforcement),

(ii) section 48 of the Freedom of Information Act 2000 (practice recommendations), or

(iii) Part IV of that Act (enforcement), or

(b) the commission of an offence under—

(i) any provision of the Data Protection Act 1998 other than paragraph 12 of Schedule 9 (obstruction of execution of warrant), or

(ii) section 77 of the Freedom of Information Act 2000 (offence of altering etc. records with intent to prevent disclosure).

(2) Nothing in Article 19(1) applies in relation to the disclosure of information in accordance with this Article."

The Commissioner for Local Administration in Scotland

13. In section 30 of the Local Government (Scotland) Act 1975 (limitation on disclosure of information), after subsection (5) there is inserted—   1975 c. 30.

"(5A) Information obtained from the Information Commissioner by virtue of section 76 of the Freedom of Information Act 2000 shall be treated for the purposes of subsection (2) as obtained for the purposes of an investigation under this Part of this Act and, in relation to such information, the reference in subsection (2)(a) to the investigation shall have effect as a reference to any investigation."

SCHEDULE 8

Section 86.

REPEALS

PART I

REPEAL COMING INTO FORCE ON PASSING OF ACT

Chapter	Short title	Extent of repeal
1998 c. 29.	The Data Protection Act 1998.	In Schedule 14, in paragraph 2(1), the words "or, if earlier, 24th October 2001".

PART II

REPEALS COMING INTO FORCE IN ACCORDANCE WITH SECTION 87(2)

Chapter	Short title	Extent of repeal
1958 c. 51.	The Public Records Act 1958.	In Schedule 1, in Part II of the Table in paragraph 3, the entry relating to the Data Protection Commissioner.
1967 c. 13.	The Parliamentary Commissioner Act 1967.	In Schedule 2, the entry relating to the Data Protection Commissioner.
1975 c. 24.	The House of Commons Disqualification Act 1975.	In Schedule 1, in Part III, the entry relating to the Data Protection Commissioner.
1975 c. 25.	The Northern Ireland Assembly Disqualification Act 1975.	In Schedule 1, in Part III, the entry relating to the Data Protection Commissioner.
1998 c. 29.	The Data Protection Act 1998.	In Schedule 5, Part III. In Schedule 15, paragraphs 1(1), 2, 4, 5(2) and 6(2)

PART III

REPEALS COMING INTO FORCE IN ACCORDANCE WITH SECTION 87(3)

Chapter	Short title	Extent of repeal
1958 c. 51.	The Public Records Act 1958.	In section 5, subsections (1), (2) and (4) and, in subsection (5), the words from "and subject to" to the end. Schedule 2.
1975 c. 24.	The House of Commons Disqualification Act 1975.	In Schedule 1, in Part II, the entry relating to the Data Protection Tribunal.
1975 c. 25.	The Northern Ireland Assembly Disqualification Act 1975.	In Schedule 1, in Part II, the entry relating to the Data Protection Tribunal.
1998 c. 29.	The Data Protection Act 1998.	In section 1(1), in the definition of "data", the word "or" at the end of paragraph (c). In Schedule 15, paragraphs 1(2) and (3), 3, 5(1) and 6(1).

Printed in the UK by The Stationery Office Limited
under the authority and superintendence of Carol Tullo, Controller of
Her Majesty's Stationery Office and Queen's Printer of Acts of Parliament